BACKWARD TO FORWARD
PROSE PIECES

MAURICE KENNY

WHITE PINE PRESS · FREDONIA, NEW YORK

Some of these pieces were first published, in a different form, by:
Bright Hill Press in *Iroquois Voices, Iroquois Visions* edited, in part by Bertha Rogers; *Confluencia; Gay Sunshine; Greenfield Review; Margins;* New York Foundation for the Arts Newsletter; St. Martins Press in *Living the Spirit* edited by Will Roscoe; *Studies in American Indian Literature;* The University of Iowa Press in *The Continuing Influence of Walt Whitman* edited by Robert K. Martin; the University of Nebraska Press in *I Tell You Now* edited by Arnold Krupat and Brian Swann; *Wacazo Sa;* and the *Wooster Review.* "Not to Forget" was a lecture delivered at Rutgers University.

Publication of this book was made possible, in part, by grants from the National Endowment for the Arts, the New York State Council on the Arts, and by the Arts Council in Buffalo & Erie County's Decentralization Program with funds from the County of Erie and the Nicholas Patterson Trust.

ISBN 1-877727-69-5

Printed and bound in the United States of America

Book design: Watershed Design

Cover photograph: Black Kettle and Chiefs in Denver—September 1864. Courtesy of the State Historical Society of Colorado.

Published by
White Pine Press
10 Village Square
Fredonia, New York 14063

CONTENTS

For
Neal Burdick, Sarah Iselin,
Carole Ashkinaze, and Brett Sanchi
and in memory of Lorne Simon

A PSEUDO-ESSAY:
SOMETIMES CALLED A PREFACE

Perhaps though not mastering the art of the essay, there is always a special thrill in gathering information and creating some sort of form out of chaos, especially since memory is so fallible. Having had the dubious honor of teaching Composition 131 for a number of semesters with no certain joy or pleasure, there has been the desire to express ideas, personal and political, in a concrete and lasting manner. At times, I've even attempted to do this with a flourish, much depending, of course, upon the magazine editor and the commission, as many of these pieces were written on commission. Often the piece, with some editing, was published, but other times a particular piece might have been rejected because it arrived too late for the slated issue, or the season was wrong, or "we just printed a piece dealing with the exact same subject in the last issue." I cannot recall a rejection ever given because of bad writing or insufficient information, because I did not check facts, or because "we simply lost interest." All in all, these compositions have provided a delightful time spent in reverie.

The essay is most creative and there is a positive response coming from Jung's collective memory in such voices as William Zinser, Charles Lamb, John Mohawk, George Orwell, D.H.

Lawrence, Rick Hill, Gretal Erhlich, Guy Davenport, Francis Parkman, Edmund Wilson, Gore Vidal, Francis Jennings, Barbara Tuchman. These essayists are greatly admired.

It was probably George Orwell's "Shooting Elephants", which kindled my need to write essays. Travel pieces have always fascinated especially those of Graham Greene and W. Somerset Maugham. Nature writing has intrigued for many years, as have all writings on Native American history, which is the same as American history, whether correct, fraudulent, inept, racist, or mere poppycock. Both in my poems and essays, making right the wrongs has been a decided goal and, I hope, a worthy achievement and success.

A number of people need to be thanked and mentioned for contributions to the creative efforts of this collection: Elaine LaMattina and Dennis Maloney; Chris Shaw; David Lampe; Carol and Joseph Bruchac; my former Advanced Composition teacher at Butler University, the late Dr. Graham; my composition students from the many semesters, particularly Emily Warner, Bill Zipse, Pia Borromeo, and "Dan," who composed a magnificent tract on bow hunting which renewed my faith in students. I must also mention a few of my suffering colleagues who also have spent much too much time at the head of an eight o'clock class teaching the art of the three-hundred word essay: John Radigan, Aaron Perkus and my ever magnificent Madge Heller. Thanks, too, to Claire Doyle, Alan Steinberg and Deborah McGill. And to encourage him to look further and deeper into the pleasures of the nature essay, I would like to thank my surrogate son, Dean Roczen, for our hundreds of chats about the flora and fauna on Maple Hill in Saranac Lake. And my gratitude to Bob Cook for a most rewarding paddle two summers ago listening to loons on Big Polliwog Pond, as well as to Brett Sanchi for his wondrous photographs of Adirondack flora and for hosting my cat, Lucy. Thanks to Jerome Rothenberg; to Alice Sharp, who helped so much at the Colorado Historical Society; to Peter Hoch and the late Alfred Hoch. Gratitude is also in order to Lynn Whalen, often my chauffeur, and Jamie Kincaid, co-worker in new ventures, and to my typist Jennifer Yarrow. And, naturally, to all the essayists for the hours of pleasure spent reading their illuminating words and for the depth of their ideas.

–Maurice Kenny
Saranac Lake, N.Y.
Summer in the Adirondacks

BACKWARD

TINSELLED BUCKS:
A HISTORICAL STUDY IN INDIAN HOMOSEXUALITY

Upon coming to the New World, Spain loosed an army of priests upon the Indians to take souls for God and gold for King. They did not record the sexual practices of the natives. Neither did the French Jesuits who first explored northeastern America, the Dutch, the English, or the Puritans. It must be recalled that pleasure-sex was branded "wrong" by civilized Europeans. In general, however, the Indian attitude toward sex was not constricting:

> Compared to white attitudes toward sex, Indians were utterly uninhibited. They suffered no embarrassment...Adults coupled freely in front of their children or anyone else. One prominent chief was often seen walking about his village naked, displaying an erection.....And the American Indian was completely innocent of the notion that something he enjoyed might be "wrong." "Wrong" would have been an incomprehensible concept to them in that context.

Homosexuality was accepted, if not condoned, within most primal societies, and the American Indian was no exception to the rule. Homosexuality was found in all American Indian tribes, though perhaps it was kept to a small number in particular tribes.

Every American Indian tribe had its fetishes and taboos, but no tribe had ironclad laws that said a young man need take this or that path; he made up his own mind and followed the direction of his "puberty vision" and his natural inclination, though the tribal mores prodded him toward the warrior-hunter career. If a youth chose not to go on the hunt or join a warrior society then he need not comply with the general pattern and war or hunt. But in his choice of not warring, he was usually compelled to forfeit his right to masculine privilege. He also possibly exposed himself to insulting ridicule and abuse though rarely would he have been castigated, ostracized, or expelled from the encampment. Should he decide war paint was against his basic nature, he could dress as a female and take her occupations. He might even become the second or third wife to a warrior or chief, should the benefactor possess sufficient wealth to support an addition to his lodge.

Alexander Henry the Younger, a trapper-trader, was an early chronicler of the Indian lifestyle, despite his aversion to the red man. In 1801 Henry wrote of "La Berdash" and left a description:

> This person is a curious compound between a man and a woman. He is a man both to members and courage, but pretends to be womanish and dresses as such. His walk and mode of sitting, his manners, occupations, and language are those of a woman. His father, who is a great chief amongst the Saulteurs, cannot persuade him to act like a man.

In her book *Male and Female,* Margaret Mead writes of the berdache: "Among many American Indian tribes the berdache, the man who dressed and lived as a woman, was a recognized social institution, counterpointed to the excessive emphasis upon bravery and hardiness for men."

Certain berdaches were celebrated, and their names and exploits have come down to us. Henry the Younger and Walter O'Meara mention Yellow Head of the Ojibway; George Bent informed anthropologist George B. Grinnell of several old Cheyenne: Pipe, Bridge (also mentioned by Mari Sandoz in *Cheyenne Autumn),* Hiding Shield Under His Robe, and Good Road Woman—names somewhat indicative of their proclivities. Stanley Vestal, the noted historian, wrote favorably, though amusingly, of a famed Arapaho medicine man, Waksenna, and how he saved his band from Asiatic cholera. Ruth Benedict refers to Matilda Coxe Stevenson's Zuni friend, We'wha.

The berdache was known by different names to different tribes. George Catlin, the painter, recorded that the Sauk and Fox tribes called the berdache *i-coo-coo-a;* the Ojibwa (Chippewa) named him *agokwa;* the Cheyenne, according to George Bird Grinnell, called him *hee-man-eh;* and the Sioux, *winkte.*

Catlin, who apparently was not deeply disturbed by the presence of berdaches in the Mandan villages, has left a long description of these young dandies. Once, excited by a young man's attire and countenance, Catlin painted a Mandan dandy. He destroyed the portrait before completion at the insistence of an indignant chief who'd had his portrait done earlier. In his *Letters and Notes* Catlin wrote:

So highly do Mandan braves and worthies value the honour of being painted; and so little do they value a man, however lavishly Nature may have bestowed her master touch upon him, who has not the pride and noble bearing of a warrior

These clean and elegant gentlemen, who are few in each tribe, are held in very little estimation by the chiefs and braves; inasmuch as it is known by all, that they have a most horrible aversion to arms, and are denominated "faint hearts" and "old women" by the whole tribe, and are therefore but little respected. They seem, however, to be tolerably well contented with the appellation, together with the celebrity they have acquired amongst the women and children for the beauty and elegance of their personal appearance....

These gay and tinselled bucks may be seen in a pleasant day in all their plumes, astride of their pied or dappled ponies, with a fan in the right hand, made of a turkey's tail—with a whip and fly-brush attached to the wrist of the same hand, and underneath them a white and beautiful and soft pleasure-saddle, ornamented with porcupine quills and ermine, parading through or lounging about the village....

There was nought about him of the terrible, and nought to shock the finest, chastest intellect.

Perhaps Catlin appreciated the berdache more than the Mandan Indians did. But although the Mandan may not have valued the berdache highly, they did respect the homosexual sufficiently that he was neither tortured by confinement nor driven to suicide, though surely humorous pranks must have been played upon him and epithets or ridicule applied.

Toleration of the berdache varied from tribe to tribe. Some

tribes, such as the Illinois, actually trained young men to become homosexuals and concubines of men. The Cheyenne and Sioux of the plains may not have purposely trained young men to become berdaches but certainly accepted homosexuals more readily than some other tribes.

In the Navajo myths a male hermaphrodite, Turquoise Boy, played a significant role in the Creation. He was known as the Bearer of the Sun. The Bearer of the Moon, White Shell Girl, was also a hermaphrodite. Turquoise Boy saved the ancient Navajos from the angry Water Buffalo who stood in their way between evolving from the Fourth to the Fifth and final world.

Winnebago tales of the prankish Trickster (often described as a coyote) contain references to transvestism. In one tale the male Trickster changes into a woman and marries a chief's son and bears children.

Even Lewis and Clark on their westerly exploration of Jefferson's Louisiana Purchase were confronted, but undisturbed, by berdaches. During the ferocious winter of 1804 they were encamped between the Mississippi and the Missouri rivers near a Mandan village. They were approached by "a number of Squars and men dressed in Squars Clothes [who] Came with Corn to sell to the men for little things."

Only a handful of years later, Catlin admiringly wrote of the "Dance to the *Berdashe*," as celebrated by the Sioux and the Sauk and Fox Indians:

> Dance to the *Berdashe* is a very funny and amusing scene, which happens once a year or oftener, as they choose, when a feast is given to the *"Berdashe,"* as he is called in French (or *I-coo-coo-a, in* their own language), who is a man dressed in woman's clothes, as

he is known to be all his life, and for extraordinary privileges which he is known to possess, he is driven to the most servile and degrading duties, which he is not allowed to escape; and he being the only one of the tribe submitting to this disgraceful degradation, is looked upon as medicine and sacred, and a feast is given him annually; and initiatory to it, a dance by those few young men of the tribe who can, as in the sketch, dance forward and publicly make their boast (without the denial of the Berdashe), that.... [Here follow three untranslatable lines in the Indian language.]

The berdache functioned within the tribe, often as medicine man, doctor, story teller, matchmaker, or leading scalp dancer. He was *sometimes* educated as a holy man, as certain taboos in particular tribes forbade their high priests to marry women and father children.

George Grinnell also describes at great length the ceremony of the Cheyenne scalp dance, for which he pays tribute to George Bent as informant:

These old time scalp dances were directed by a little group of men called *Hee-man-eh,* "halfmen-half-women," who usually dressed as old men....They were very popular and especial favorites of the young people, whether married or not, for they were noted matchmakers. They were fine love talkers. If a man wanted to get a girl to run away with him and could get one of these people to help him, he seldom failed. When a young man wanted to send gifts for a young woman, one of these halfmen-halfwomen was sent to the girl's relative to do the talking in making the marriage....

When a war party was preparing to start out, one of these persons was often asked to accompany it, and, in fact, in old times large war parties rarely started without one or two of them. They were good company and fine talkers. When they went with the war parties they were well treated. They watched all that was being done, and in the fighting cared for the wounded, in which they were skillful, for they were doctors or medicine men.

They were probably also assigned the task of disemboweling the enemy dead and emasculating the prone corpses. It is easily understood why a *hee-man-eh,* or halfman-halfwoman, would be chosen as leader of the scalp dance and to officiate as bearer of the scalps to the village. He had special powers, or privileged medicine, and for all intents and purposes he had if not the outer apparel then the inner spirit of both male and female. He was also clean of the menstrual taboo. Mountain Wolf Woman, a Winnebago, related in her autobiography that while in her period a woman "should not look at anyone, not even a glance. If you look at a man you will contaminate his blood. Even a glance will cause you to be an evil person."

In his book *The Cheyennes,* E. Adamson Hoebel suggests that the fact that enemy scalps were given to the *hee-man-eh* "indicates that warriors feel their success is due to the presence of these personages" in victorious battle. "War parties like to have Halfmen-halfwomen along, not only for their medical skill, but because they are socially graceful and entertaining."

A note might be added here that women were rarely taken on war parties because should a menstrual flow come upon a woman, her blood might very well bring defeat upon the party due to her impurity. A series of long purification rites would result, causing delay that could end in dishonorable defeat. Males lived in great fear of the female process. As females did not accompany the war party, a *hee-man-eh* would easily serve for sexual entertainments, as it was well known to the elders that young hot-headed braves' frustration might result in either a disorderly attack or a sophomoric group raiding an enemy for first honors before the war chief could assemble the more mature and total war party. Young men, especially those courting maidens, were constantly running off from the main party to count first coup and take honors to lay at their lovers' feet for her respect and eventually her hand in marriage. No young girl wished to marry a brave who came to her without war honors, a first feather, or a proud wound. Hence the potential need of a *hee-man-eh* to cool youthful foolishness.

Colonel Richard Irving Dodge, in the 1880s, wrote of a special social dance during which a pretty girl of the Cheyenne village had captivated the eyes and hearts of most attending males. Dodge subtitles the episode "A Delicious Bit of Masquerading": "Finally, a young buck with whom she was dancing discovered that 'she' was a boy dressed in his sister's clothing. The little rascal had played his part so well as to mystify the whole party for half the night, and with so pretty, sprightly, and natural an action, that half the bucks in the dance had made love to him. It was considered a wonderful feat, and made great sport." Dodge wrote, as did Paul Radin, that the male Indian considered affection effeminate.

There is little in journals, chronicles, histories, or anthropological studies relating to lovemaking between two Indian males, but the many references to the berdache certainly indicate that copulation was practiced. However, the berdache, unlike captives, especially women, rarely suffered the experience of rape and the act of being "passed on the plains"—that is, attacked *en masse.*

Walter O'Meara cites an example of unrequited love between a young Ojibwa *agokwa* and the mountaineer John Tanner. He was Yellow Head, the same *agokwa* who had so greatly perturbed Alexander Henry the Younger.

One winter while Tanner was encamped at a post on Red-River in the central north, a son of a celebrated Ojibwa chief visited the post. Tanner termed him a "creature." He claimed that most, if not all, Indian tribes had *agokwas.* The Ojibwa accepted the berdache. Yellow Head took a fancy to the white man and set his stars upon capturing Tanner as his lover. To Tanner, who had sometime before married an Indian maid and sired children by her, the "creature" was a loathsome object. The *agokwa* offered himself to Tanner, and he was not discouraged by the mountaineer's rejection. The females of the post took great amusement in this odd affair and, most likely, prodded the *agokwa* to further and more intimate advances, which Tanner spurned and nipped in the bud.

Yellow Head disappeared for a few days. Tanner felt tremendous relief and decided he had finally chased the "creature" off. But the berdache returned to the post later with a pack horse loaded with fresh meat. At that time the post was low on supplies, especially fresh meat, and the people were hungry. Normally under those circumstances meat would have gained a hunter access to a maid's lodge and bed. But neither fresh meat nor the hunter's prowess won Yellow Head Tanner's love or male body. Yellow Head, the *agokwa,* received instead total rejection for his generous and strenuous efforts. A solution was discovered at last. The chief, Wagetote, already served by two wives, married the *agokwa.* Tanner was saved from his embarrassment and the trauma of either ridding himself of the determined berdache or accepting Yellow Head into his lodge as concubine or wife. But love between two males, of either race, was not always unrequited. It can be assumed that there were exceptions that led to romance and marriage. All males did not have Tanner's aversion to *agokwas* and the comforts they might bring to a tired warrior-hunter.

Even when he sometimes wore female garb, the berdache was not always a fluttering "sissy." A number of males who practiced homosexuality were fierce warriors and were not effeminate, transvestite homoerotics. Bestiality was sometimes practiced, and sex with a recently killed enemy was not frowned upon in certain tribes. What greater ridicule or humiliation in defeat could be put upon a foe! His macho powers would be weakened in the Spirit World.

Henry Rowe Schoolcraft, who had personally known Yellow Head, reported that he was very courageous in battle and told of his exploits and daring on the warpath. Yellow Head was, according to O'Meara, "famous for having once stood off a whole band of Sioux with nothing but a bow and arrows, while he covered his companions' retreat to safety."

John Major Hurdy wrote in his book *American Indian Religion:*

> However, the desire to copulate with one's sex is by no means connected, as army men in every culture have witnessed, with timidity in battle.... Society worked effectively to prevent individual guilt, so also

its structure mitigated against the development of machoism....Lakota males have been known to commit suicide rather than accept the fate their vision and inner reactions told them was theirs....The degree of physical courage, superb skill, and keen competitive spirit demanded by the masculine ideal was so high that not all males were capable of conforming to it. Those who were clumsy or weak, or were cursed with sluggish reflexes, rarely survived to become problems as adults. And for those who cringed at violence, Sioux society provided an escape route.

The cult of the berdache was more known on the western plains within the Sioux (Lakota) and Cheyenne tribes west of the Mississippi than in other areas of America. There is no particularly good reason why this should be true other than the possibility that these were large and powerful tribes before the white man decimated their numbers. Within such large groups a social-religious use could be found for the berdache. As there were sufficient warriors and hunters to both protect and feed the community, some males were allowed to pursue more gentle endeavors. A more leisurely society could afford such deviations from the straight path of war and the hunt, as medicine men to provide the stimulus of religion, and as artisans. A youth not inclined to the warpath or game hunting might spend his life in pursuit of other careers and was not necessarily required to propagate the race. The tribe could afford to allow a youth the lifestyle of a berdache. In the Southwest, homosexuality, along with slavery, was known and condoned in such tribes as the Navajo and Mojave. Margaret Mead's observation regarding "the conspicuous transvestism of the Mojave—where the transvestite men mimic pregnancy and childbirth, going aside from the camp to be ceremonially delivered of stones" attests to its presence in the desert lands. The Far West, the South, and the Northeast certainly were not without such personages.

It is known that the Indian berdache sometimes married their own sex and lived together, and the "husband" was not always a fellow invert. Throughout any discussion of Indian homosexuality it must be remembered that the cardinal aim and fulfillment of Indian males was the attainment of honor and glory on the warpath. From birth this was instilled and impressed daily upon his mind. Masculine strength was the protector of life and liberty; the provider-hunter sustained the people, and procreation was the basic sexual drive. If too many "faint hearts" were allowed to survive, the tribe and culture were doomed. For this reason small boys were sometimes taken from the mother, who might shed too much love and attention and sway the teetering balance of a boy 's potential inversion, at a very early age, usually before they attained five years. In some Indian nations, the male child was given to an uncle to rear in the respected masculine custom and Indian way. This was a safeguard to eliminate the possibility that a boy would turn from the warrior and hunter's gun. Needless to say, occasionally a male slipped through this protective measure and matured a berdache to denounce the warpath and accept female clothes and drudgery. Not all males could meet the high Indian standards of masculinity: physically malformed men were often obliged to assume maiden ways.

A number of contemporary novels, such as Thomas Berger's excellent *Little Big Man,* a satire of the West, treat romance between Indian males. Berger's satire fails only because he himself became entangled with his characters and took too serious an interest in their lives and conflicts, even probably those of the young *hee-man-eh,* Little Horse, who Berger stripped of masculine attire and lifestyle and costumed in a female's deerskin tunic. Berger gave Little Horse a husband and a certain amount of joy in the union. Even though placed in the novel for comic relief, Little Horse fared better than most of the other principal characters, including the hero, Jack Crabb. *Little Big Man,* an important major novel of the twentieth century, is a highly researched account of Cheyenne life and death during the mid 1800s. Though Berger's satire is not completely satisfactory, his power of vision is ovewhelming, his humor delightfully entertaining, and his characters' conflicts humanly moving:

> If a Cheyenne don't believe he can stand a man's life, he ain't forced to. He can become a *heemaneh,* which is to say half-man, half-woman. There are uses for these fellows and everybody likes them. They are sometimes chemists, specializing in making of the love-potions, and generally good entertainers. They wear women's clothes and can get married to another man, if such be his taste....
>
> My other foster-brother, Little Horse, dressed like a Cheyenne woman, came in and entertained us with very graceful singing and dancing. It did my heart good to see he made such a success of being a *hee-maneh.*

Little Horse chose to marry Younger Bear of the Contraries, or the Bowstring Warrior Society. The Contrary warriors were a very special society. If in the "puberty vision" a youth is visited by the Thunderbirds (Hawks)—and it is the intercession of this sign that designates a boy's future occupation within the tribal arts of war, hunt, medicine, and so on—he becomes a suicidal warrior. He may not marry a female. If he does marry he must forfeit his lance, inherent with sexual symbolism that suggests the male sex organ tied and restrained. Every thought, word, and action he commits must be accomplished backward. If in reality he is hungry he must feel contented. He bathes in sand and dries off with water. He cries when he is happy and laughs when sorrowful. He rejects heterosexuality. He is obliged, by taboo and his society, to do everything in opposites. This rejection of heterosexuality-could lead only to male love. There were usually only two or three Contraries to a band, deviates in their own right, often accompanied by *hee-man-ehs*.

Berger's *hee-man-eh,* Little Horse, married such a young Contrary. Younger Bear sold his Thunder-Bow, which allowed marriage between them. Berger cannot resist a play for humor, a stab at jest: "So when the Bear was all dressed and looking at me, I couldn't forbear from needling him a little, for though nobody among the Cheyenne ever condemns a *hee-man-eh,* it is O.K. to rib the fellow he lives with."

In one stroke Berger sums up the Cheyenne traditional attitude toward homosexuality and transvestism. His conclusion may very well speak for other Indian tribes, as well. As Ruth Benedict, in reference to the Zuni Indians of New Mexico, wrote in her book *Patterns of Culture*:

> Social scorn, however, was not visited upon the berdache but upon the man he chose to live with him. The latter was regarded as a weak man who had chosen an easy berth instead of the recognized goals of their culture; he did not contribute to the household, which was already a model for all households

through the sole efforts of the berdache. His sexual adjustment was not singled out in the judgment that was passed upon him, but in terms of his economic adjustment he was an outcast.

The contemporary Cheyenne, especially a reservation-oriented Cheyenne, might not accept Berger's or Benedict's statements. The modern Indian has been programmed by white society so that his former mores and measurements have been changed to fit his ever-assimilating environment. With the loss of his religious rites and culture, there is probably no place for the contemporary *hee-man-eh* within that social structure. There are no warriors to entertain on the warpath; no scalps to dance over; no mountaineers to court, subdue, and copulate with; and certainly no ceremonial dances exclusively devoted to the berdache. Many traditionalists have become racist and sexist, and are generally disquieted when among homosexuals. Hollywood, TV, and the church have had a heavy influence on the changing attitude of Indian thought.

Berger was writing fictionally of a "romantic" past, and, though accurately researched, *Little Big Man* may represent one man's point of view. Perhaps even today, the reservation Indian still fears the possibility of ridicule, as Paul Radin suggested in reference to his Winnebago at the turn of the century. Though a homosexual may not be a Trickster, he is in certain quarters regarded as a buffoon to be laughed at, mimicked, jeered, and even possibly scorned.

Frederick Manfred, in his western novels, has various references to homosexuality, again in a humorous, jesting vein, or as a curse or epithet spat by a female upon her lazy husband. In *Lord Grizzly,* Manfred refers to a berdache as he who "Can't

Father."

Non-Indians, or Anglos, were not the only writers on male love in Indian societies. The Indian himself wrote, though often with the help, aid, and tape recorders of such white men as John G. Neihardt, who was responsible for the important story of the holy man, Black Elk, and Thomas B. Marquis, who helped direct the Cheyenne warrior Wooden Leg to express his life story. Richard Erdoes taped and edited the life of the Lakota medicine man John Fire, or Lame Deer, an old man still living in 1972, when his book, *Lame Deer, Seeker of Visions,* was first published.

John Lame Deer, with Erdoes, stopped for a drink in a country bar. Near them on a stool sat a man, obviously "gay." Lame Deer opened a conversation with the man:

> He told me that a *winkte* has a gift of prophesy and that he himself could predict the weather....In our tribe we go to a *winkte* to give a newborn child a secret name....A name given by a *winkte* is supposed to bring its bearer luck and long life. In the old days it was worth a fine horse—at the least....
>
> We think if a woman has two little ones growing inside of her, if she is going to have twins, sometimes instead of giving birth to two babies they have formed up in her womb into just one, into a half man-half woman kind of being. We call such a person a *winkte.* He could be a hermaphrodite with male and female parts....To us a man is what nature, or his dreams, makes him. We accept him for what he wants to be. That's up to him. Still, fathers did not like to see their boys hanging around a *winkte's* place and told them to stay away.

The Sioux *winkte* still exist. As the half man-half woman that Lame Deer spoke with said, "If nature puts a burden on a man by making him different, it also gives him a power."

According to Erdoes, the Sioux had an old custom of giving themselves secret names divulged to no one. Only the donor and the recipient knew the name. The name given by the *winkte* was sort of a good-luck talisman, and apparently the names received are "very sexy, even funny, very outspoken." Were they to be known they would cause embarrassment and a great deal of jest. Lame Deer named Sitting Bull, Black Elk, and the famed Crazy Horse as bearers of these secret *winkte* names. The names could make one famous. "Well, this man-woman told me that in the old days the *winktes* used to call each other sisters and had a special hill where they were buried. I asked him when he died, when he went south, what he would be in the spirit land, a man or a woman. He told me he would be both. It was a long interview, lasting through two bottles of wine."

A melancholy permeates John Lame Deer's words, even within the trace of humor, a nostalgic bending toward the traditional past, the glory, the freedom that can never again be known by the Indian. Recently a middle-aged Navajo berdache said that he was not accepted in the off-reservation world, but while living with his people, the traditional Navajos, he is paid respect because it was the berdache who kept the men and women, the people, together as a unit, a tribe. He may have been referring to the Turquoise Boy, the hermaphrodite who helped bring the Navajos into the fifth and present world. This man, an off-reservation transvestite who is no longer revered in ceremony, insists that Indians condone homosexuality. Other young Indians, members of Gay American Indians, have organized in San Francisco to fight the current ignorance and abuse directed toward them by their own reservation brothers and sisters. Perhaps when Indians have once again regained their old cultures, languages, and ceremonies, the berdache not only will be respected but will find a place in his chosen society. The current taboos against his nature will then have changed sufficiently so that he may make a contribution to and function once more in that reorganized culture.

Black Charlotte

There is not much left of Bent's Fort, now a National Historic Site in southeastern Colorado, except the adobe foundations, an inch or so high. The river has been shifted, and grass, thick and green from heavy spring rains, has reclaimed the land. Cottonwoods grow in abundance, offering shade and food to a populous beaver colony. Rabbits, skunks, and coyotes prowl the grounds at night unmolested and, off in the distance, a forest protects a few deer. Some wildflowers can be found nearby— blue columbine, fleabane, locoweed—and fall-ripened berries drop from the bush. Hawks, buzzards, and magpies, among other birds, can be seen wheeling the skies, but there is neither Indian, trader, trapper, nor cavalry officer in sight to tell the tales of a hundred and fifty years ago.

Yet in 1846, that year of expansion, a mighty contingent of people passed through this part of the Arkansas River valley. The young and sickly Francis Parkman who had been wandering the Oregon Trail seeking authentic Indians in preparing for his histories of North America, dipped down to the Arkansas. The seventeen year old Lewis H. Garrard was already on the river living in a Cheyenne village, chasing buffalo, and making retaliatory raids on the hostile Pueblos of Taos. General Stephen Watts Kearny was entrenched at Bent's Fort, using it as a base for an invasion of the Mexican territory, and the Bents themselves were doing a fair business.

The famous and infamous, the nothings of the buffalo wallows and the mighty of the plains, rolled into Bent's Fort. Josiah Gregg had already, before 1846, made his pilgrimage to the garrison and had written his story in the marvelous *Commerce of the Prairies*. Practically everyone of importance in the west made at least a night's stopover at the Bent brothers' fort. James P. Beckwith, the mulatto mountainman who had lived with the Crow and had allegedly been made a chief of that Nation, was often within the confines of the adobe fortress. Kit Carson, famed "Indian killer," worked eight years at the fort, supplying the kitchen with thousands of pounds of buffalo meat. Colonel John C. Fremont, with his chronicler, the artist Soloman Carvalho, and the able Lt. J. W. Abert, a topographer, had stopped briefly on their trail of exploration into California. It was there that Fremont hired Carson to join the command as scout. Certainly many famous trappers, including Sublette and Maxwell, took a night's rest and a cup of boiled coffee there. George Frederick Ruxton, the English sportsman, was there in '46 and, according to the account in his *In the Old West*, sampled a "feast upon the best provender the game-covered country affords." There is little doubt that George Catlin, the now internationally known painter of Indians, had paid a call on the Bents, or that Baptiste Charbonneau, son of the famed "bird woman," Sacajawea, chewed off a tobacco cud between the walls of the fort.

Abert described the fort as:

> ...composed of a series of rooms resembling casements and forming a hollow square...A round tower on the left, as you enter, and another diago-

nally opposite, constitute the flanking arrangements. The outer walls, which are nearly two feet in thickness, intersect...the outside walls of the enciente and towers, pierced with loop holes, are continued four feet above the flat roofs...The coping of the wall is planted with cacti, which bear red and white flowers."

In the mid-1830s Charles and William Bent had brought to their fort three slaves from their home in St. Louis: a Mr. and Mrs. Dick (Charlotte) Green and Dick's brother, Andrew. Dick spent the major portion of his time in New Mexico with Charles, who had been named provisional governor of the territory. Andrew served the Bents in various ways and was often persuaded to don the uniform of butler. He could be seen carrying trays of frosty tumblers of mint juleps to the master of the house when he was entertaining guests in his private quarters on the second floor. Charlotte Green was made head cook of the trading post/garrison, and soon her cooking expertise spread her name throughout the wilderness. In his 1915 book, *In the Old West*, Ruxton remarked that Charlotte Green "was celebrated from Long's Peak to the Cumbre Espanola for flapjacks and pumpkin pie."

The young and pretty Susan Magoffin arrived at the fort in a wagon train with her husband , Samuel, in 1846. On July 27, she commented in her diary:

And now for something of a description. Well the outside exactly fills my idea of an ancient castle. It is built of adobes, unburned brick, and Mexican style so far. The walls are very high and very thick with rounding corners. There is but one entrance, this is to the east rather.

In reality, this "ancient castle" was an imposing structure rising from the floor of the flat plains. There were some twenty odd rooms to the fort, three of which were practically the sole province of Charlotte, who soon came to be known on the plains as "Black Charlotte." Her three rooms, on entering the east facing gate, were on the left beyond the council room and walled off from the inner corral. It is amazing that of the ruins, her kitchen seems to be the best preserved.

Arriving only a few weeks before the Magoffins, an exhausted and ill Parkman had made the following notes in his journal:

> Bent's Fort stands on the river about seventy miles below the Pueblo...it is visible for a considerable distance, standing with its high clay walls in the midst of the scorching plains. The grass for miles around was cropped close by the horses of General Kearny's soldiery. When we came to the fort, we found that not only had the horses eaten up the grass, but their owners had made away with the stores of the little trading post so that we had great difficulty in procuring the few articles which we required for our homeward journey. The army was gone, the life and bustle passed away, and the fort was a scene of dull and lazy tranquility...The proprietors were absent, and we were received by Mr. Hod, who had been left in charge of the fort. He invited us to dinner, where to our admiration, we found a table laid with a white cloth, with castors in the middle, and chairs in

place around it.

Parkman was not the only visitor astonished by the table "laid with a white cloth." Many an Eastern adventurer or weary man down from mountain trapping, away from proper dining civilities for months, possibly years, found this domestic scene not merely unexpected but a sweet comfort.

It is more than likely that Charlotte spread the white table cloth, placed the castors in the middle of the table, and placed chairs around it. As Ruxton recorded in *In the Old West,* she loved to call out to all and sundry, "I'm de only lady in de damn Injun country." It is not too much to conjecture that she had either brought the white cloth along on her emigration from St. Louis or had cajoled the Bents into procuring one. Surely the famous white cloth was not so much to make the mountain men feel at home but to impress the few other females of the fort or the ladies who stopped off on the long trek west.

A detailed, accurate description of Charlotte has not come down to us, but by putting bits and pieces together it may be assumed that she was neither old nor a teenager. Ruxton speaks of her as being "a fair lady of color." As other women of the fort, including half-bloods and Mexicans, have been described as being fat and ugly or greasy and skinny, it is reasonable to assume she was at least average. Some quality creeps across time, some touch of personality, charisma, wavers out of ghostly shadows and suggests that she might well have been an attractive woman. William Bent, called the Little White Chief because of his short stature, had an eye for women, and Charlotte seems to have had a persuasive upper-hand with him. Was her attractiveness the weapon she held over the little master of the fort? Was it her genius over the woodstove, or both?

Susan Magoffin, only eighteen at the time of her visit to the fort, had a clear eye for observation and little that went on in the fort failed to attract her attention. She harshly describes some of the females of the fort, although she concludes that the "Fort is not such a bad place after all. There are some good people in and about it as well as in other places." She managed to take in the kitchen and dining room with a sweep of her glance, although she and her husband took their meals in private quarters above the plaza. But Mrs. Magoffin fails to add even a footnote to her diary that mentions Black Charlotte, who had to have loomed very large within the fort's motley group. Add to this the fact that Charlotte was one of the few English-speaking women in "de damn Injun country," and it would be expected that one or the other would seek acquaintance. Susan Magoffin fell dangerously ill during her visit to the fort and was confined to her upstairs bedroom. Charlotte must have paid a call on the sick room, but there is no mention of this in the diary. Perhaps the call was made, or service rendered, while Mrs. Magoffin was delirious with fever and unaware of the visit. Or perhaps Susan Magoffin, Kentucky born and raised, had not been away from the South long enough to have dropped prejudices. Or, being a lady of means used to having servants in attendance, perhaps she did not find a black woman about the house, even on the deserted plains, unusual enough to deserve comment. Perhaps her rigid background did not allow social contact.

Though Charlotte Green failed to attract the attention of the haughty Susan Magoffin, she did not fail in catching the curious and sprightly glances of the less gentle folk of the fort. Surely the Indians, of both sexes, found her a fantastic creature, one to stand slightly back from since she might possess great magical powers, being a black-white woman. The men loved her. They enjoyed both her company and her food. Lewis H. Garrard, in *Wah-To-Yah and the Oregon Trail* (University of Oklahoma, 1962) describes himself "with numbed fingers gradually thawing in the long low dining room, drinking hot coffee, eating bread, butter and 'State's doin's' and listening to Charlotte, the glib-tongued, sable fort cook, retailing [sic] her stock of news and surmises..."

Stanley Vestal retold a kitchen scene in *The Old Santa Fe Trail* (Bantam Books, 1957):

> Best of all to the men hungry for civilized food was the kitchen from whose window floated the welcome aroma of boiling coffee and bread making. A little flattery of the Negress in charge...might persuade black Charlotte to part with a pie or some of her delicious biscuits, the only biscuits between Westport and California. Those who were fortunate enough to be invited to dinner enjoyed the unfamiliar luxury of putting their knees under a table covered with a white cloth and adorned with castors. There a man might well remember how a fork was used, and eat...from a tin plate like a gentleman.

Naturally, the fort having Herculean tasks in cooking, Charlotte would have had help in her kitchen, Mexican women or half-bloods, while she stood off, steward, chef, and manager, directing the ingredients for the "state's doin's." She most likely supervised a garden from whence came the pumpkins to make her famous pies.

Though her service as cook was her main function, her talents as dancer and belle of the ball were not only needed but deeply appreciated by the male population. In *The Old Santa Fe Trail*, Vestal writes:

Sometimes, a fandango was held in the fort when

a caravan corralled there. In that case, the fiddler mounted the table and the old heart square dance filled the crowded room with dust up to the ceiling. Chipita, the enormously fat housekeeper, flopped about with colossal good humor. The Indian squaws pranced, giggling without a trace of Indian stoicism, and Black Charlotte aped the fine ladies whom she had seen pass on their way to California. Women were so few that everyone received the most flattering attention.

At Christmas there was usuallly an all night ball when the half-blood Rosalie, common-law wife of William's carpenter, Frenchman Ed, and Black Charlotte, dressed in their best, with earrings and bracelets clattering, took all favors and honors from the other women on the post. No woman was a match for Charlotte's dancing, possessing neither her exuberance nor light foot. Garrard spends a full fifteen lines describing her gaily dancing the fandango to the tune of squeaking fiddles.

Since so few women lived at the fort, it is not unreasonable to assume that Charlotte and the others were frequently swung joyously around the Bents' buffalo robe press, which stood in the center of the quadrangle, tripping the light fantastic with a grizzled trapper down from many months in the mountains. Although her husband was off in New Mexico, there is nothing to suggest that Charlotte failed to observe her marriage vows, although she perhaps had to fight off more that one male who, staggering from whiskey, mistook her friendliness, congenial spirit and exuberance for an invitation to the pleasures of the bed. She remained childless throughout her years at the fort, where she enjoyed a measure of freedom and pleasure few other women of her era ever knew.

Following the murder of Charles Bent at Taos Pueblo, Dick Green, along with the young Garrard and Kit Carson, enterd Taos for revenge upon the heinous mutilation of their friend. For Dick's daring and valorous deeds, William granted Dick and Charlotte their freedom. Garrard, traveling eastward toward his home, encountered their caravan along the trail and discovered the Greens enroute to St. Louis. He bid them both a second, sad and final goodbye: "Charlotte, the cook also griningly showed her ivory as I extended my hands." They exchanged a bit of gossip, much to Charlotte's delight. Rosalie had run off with another member of Bent's company, Charlotte informed Garrard. Ed was with the present caravan, broken-hearted over the loss of his fiery *senorita*. The caravans parted, and nothing further is known about Black Charlotte.

Today, forty feet from the ruins of Wiliam Bent's magnificent "ancient castle," lies buried the trash of over a century ago. In the dump you might find a shard of pottery that Charlotte broke during a fracas in her kitchen in 1846. Or you may come upon a red or green bead that a belle lost whirling in the height of joy at a Christmas fandango of many years ago. Drop the bangle in your pocket—a souvenir of the "only damn lady in de Injun country." Charlotte would want you to have it to remember her by.

Yellow Wolf: The Indian Who Would Farm

Yellow Wolf lived in the vast lands west of the Black Hills of the Dakotas with his people, the Cheyenne. As a youth, he had gone to those Sacred Hills to fast and pray for the vision which would permit him to return to his village and take his place as a warrior. Among the tribes of the western plains, raids were not conducted for blood or the death of an enemy but for spoils: horses, ornaments, and honor. Tribal war did sometimes lead to the spilling of blood and a desire for revenge, but this was often avoided by a peaceful council between chiefs where important gifts were exchanged. Until the white man's arrival, war was a ceremonial sport that helped give reason to the nomadic life of the plains people, who followed the migration of the buffalo, and Yellow Wolf quickly earned honor and a herd of fine horses in raids on enemy villages.

Sometime around 1826, a war party of Gros Ventre and Blackfeet entered Yellow Wolf's village. At the campfire that night they announced that they were the bravest warriors and were headed south to hunting lands of the Kiowa and Comanche where they planned to raid and steal horses. After the boastful guests left, Yellow Wolf called a large group of people together and moved a small village into the southern tier of the plains, the Arkansas River Valley. This was the first time in tribal history that the Cheyenne had moved a permanent village so far south. Victorious raids were carried out against the Comanche and Kiowa, and the Cheyenne enriched their pony herds and piled up honors.

South of the Platte, between the North Platte and the Arkansas Rivers, Yellow Wolf's wife raised her lodgepoles and tended their son, Red Sun. They enjoyed a good life there. Buffalo, antelope, deer, and fowl were abundant; rivers offered clear waters for drinking and bathing; the earth provided a good, scavanged crop of roots, and the villages of the Kiowa , Commanche and Ute further west presented opportunities for pony raids.

Even when the "pale eyes" arrived and discovered the thick buffalo grasses of the plains, there was still plenty for all. The Cheyenne welcomed these strangers and arranged feasts where presents were exchanged. Yellow Wolf, by now chief of his band, was acutely aware of the advantages a strong friendship with these people would bring, and he enjoyed their company, their whiskey, the music of their fiddles, and the gifts of blankets, rifles, cooking pots, sugar and coffee, which came to be known as "black soup."

In the 1830s, the four Bent brothers and Ceran St. Vrain, white traders, arrived in the Upper Arkansas River Valley. When they met Yellow Wolf, he suggested that they build a permanent trading post near the buffalo range, a location best suited to trading with the various nations of the region. The young chief promised the brothers he would bring his people to their new fort, envisioning a good and profitable relationship. Donald Berthrong writes in *The Southern Cheyenne* (University of Oklahoma, 1963) that Bent's Fort was begun around 1833, with construction completed the following year. David Lavender expands the story of the friendship and trade partnership between this handful of white men destined to change the definition of wilderness and the Indian chief Yellow Wolf, all of whom sought a permanent and convivial peace:

> Charles [Bent] tried to explain the proposed fort to the Indians. Big Medicine. They popped their hands over their mouths in awe. Good, good. But not, Yellow Wolf said, properly located.
>
> Why not build the new fort in the Big Timbers, a long belt of noble cottonwoods some twenty-five miles or so down the river from the mouth of the Purgatoire? It was a favorite camping spot of such Cheyennes as dared venture that close to Comanche territory. There were shelter, good feed for ponies, plenty of firewood. Buffalo were thick. The warriors could provide, and the women tan, as many hides as the Long Knives had goods to buy.

A fort at that location would provide protection against attack by the Comanches, and perhaps Yellow Wolf believed that he was outsmarting these "pale eyes," but his integrity should not be doubted. Under his guidance, the comradeship between the Cheyenne and the Bent-St. Vrain partnership built into mutual trust, good trade, protection, and lasting friendship. William Bent married Owl Woman, daughter of Grey Thunder, Cheyenne Keeper of the Sacred Arrows, and they had a number of children over the years. Until the day of his death in 1869, William Bent fought for the rights, dignity, and lives of "his people." But not even George Bent could possibly have predicted the bloody future.

Bent often fed the Cheyenne when they were starving in later years due to the buffalo moving on when emigrants and farmers arrived. He also issued them guns for the hunt and implements for farming when the government refused, after repeated requests by various chiefs and Indian agents, to ensure the survival of their people. His behavior is not strange in light of the fact that in its long history of occupation a shot was never fired against Bent's fort nor did an arrow bite into its tall wooden gates. In the forlorn wilderness, friendship was nothing to toss lightly aside. It was precious. It did not take deep thought for the Bents to realize that without the friendship and alliance of Yellow Wolf's Cheyenne they, as traders, could expect a short duration for their lucrative business. The fort would not long exist in that dangerously rugged country: both human and natural elements would drive them back to the great Mississippi River. There is no doubt that the Indian Nations in the vicinity, would have done quite nicely without the Bents: mirrors and beads were not necessary for survival.

But invasion from the eastern seaboard was inevitable. The Bent brothers and Ceran St. Vrain only forestalled the ultimate destruction of a pure traditional life, the Indian way, and the dissemination of the plains people. Once the dark cloud of the white man's dust rose and spread across the land, it became apparent to Yellow Wolf and others of his clan that somewhere in the maze someone must be sought and begged to extend an arm of salvation. Extermination was not merely imminent but already implemented: the Iroquois, the Delaware, the Ottawa, and nearly all the other eastern, woodland Indian nations had felt the tramp of European progress. They were burying their dead and forgetting their war songs and the very language which established them as a people of a common tongue, a common her-

45

itage, a common future.

Although Yellow Wolf, in conjunction with the Bents and St. Vrain, played a major role in opening the west and to the eventual destruction of the Cheyenne nation, he never dreamed the extent of the white man's greed. Even the Bents were dismayed, sullen, and angry over the ensuing events.

1846 was a bad year for the Southern Cheyenne, a year that signaled decision and decline and touched off the first sparks of hostility toward the invading white man intent upon conquering the West. Texas had declared itself independent of Mexico in 1836 and was annexed to the United States in 1845. President Polk, who wanted also to acquire California, was glad to make use of the Texan claim to all the territory as far south and west as the Rio Grande, and the Indians of the area watched as troops plodded across their lands to fight in this Mexican War. When General Stephen Kearny and his massive army made camp at the edge of Bent's walls, warriors and chiefs watched in fear. Reports soon reached Yellow Wolf and his tribe that Kearny's troops had seized land all the way to the north shore of the Rio Grande. How many Mexican and Indian lives had been taken could not be ascertained, but the Cheyenne began to realize the magnitude of the white man's greed. Yellow Wolf's old friend, Charles Bent, was appointed provisional governor of the new territory.

In 1847, the Pueblo Indians at Taos revolted, and in the confusion Bent was murdered in his bed. A group of fifty volunteers gathered and marched on the Pueblos, and many Indians were killed. Yellow Wolf's first sympathy was with his old friend, and, in fact, he offered a war party of his own warriors to fight the Pueblo in revenge for the murder of his white brother. Yet Yellow Wolf could not help but think that too many Indians had been wantonly killed, perhaps innocent women and children. Fear moved deeper into the Cheyenne heart.

Skirmishes broke out between the plains tribes, with each faction blaming the other for alleged attacks upon the newly-arrived white settlers and cavalry troops. The presence of the Delaware, who had been removed from their Eastern homeland by the federal government, caused additional problems. Constant bickering and horse raids ensued until blood at last was spilled. Trade at the fort suffered until William Bent arranged an armistice between the Cheyenne and the Delaware. The Kiowa and Comanche were also appeased, but jealousies between these nations continued for many years.

The Cheyenne population had begun to decrease, brought down not only by firearms but by disease and alcohol. Tuberculosis, cholera, and smallpox, the diseases of the "pale eyes," took a heavy toll on the Indians, as did the famed "fire water." In no time at all, the Cheyenne became a nation of drunkards and would sell a horse or a young daughter for a jug.

As the emigrants arrived in the West, they felled what precious few cottonwoods there were along the river and creek banks. They plowed under roots and wild berries, and buffalo—frightened by the smell of the white man and his guns—moved away. Pangs of hunger began to gnaw the bellies of the Cheyenne.

It was then that Yellow Wolf, now an old man, recalled the stories of days past when the Cheyenne lived far to the northeast where strong winds whistled and snow blew. There the people had tended gardens. They ate berries and nuts, game of wild turkey and deer, and raised corn and squash in their own well-kept gardens. In those ancient days, so hidden in shadow that no living man could really remember them, the Cheyenne had lived in permanent lodges and fished the streams. That was before *pte,* the buffalo, came from the dark hole in the earth, before Buffalo

Woman brought the people to *pte*'s home on the plains.

Yellow Wolf's thoughts bent down into the darkness of that past, into the shadows, and into the voices that echoed over the rim of the living world. He knew then what he must do, and he devised a way to save his people from starvation and extinction. The white man had come into the Indians' country with little more than the clothes on his back and a rifle in his hand. Now he was happy, fat, and rich. He had first built a sod hut, then a log house; a stone village followed. He took a sharp pole and tore up the earth. In spring, green leaves poked slender tongues through the soil of the plains. In the moon of falling leaves, he gathered roots and fruit. There was not only the flesh of buffalo in the springhouse but also of elk and deer. There, too, was the flesh of cattle and pigs they had raised. Yes. His people must farm, as in ancient times. They would be warm within their lodges and food would be plentiful. Peace between the "black eyes" and the "pale eyes" would be ensured, and the Cheyenne would survive. Yellow Wolf approached J. W. Abert, a lieutenant in John Charles Fremont's exploratory force, which was spending two weeks at Bent's Fort. Through interpreters, the determined chief made known his fears of the trouble which would result in the deaths of many people and of his vision of a future with his people as farmers, which would abort inevitable tragedy. He knew that the old way was doomed. The buffalo were on their way home to darkness in the earth, and the people would perish. Donald Berthrong wrote in *The Southern Cheyenne* (University of Oklahoma, 1963):

> To prevent tribal extinction, Yellow Wolf proposed that the United States aid the Cheyennes in changing their means of subsistence. He sug-

48

gested that the government build a protecting
fort, give all adult males a mule, teach them to
cultivate the land and raise cattle.

Naturally, the Cheyenne—especially the young warriors who had
yet to win honors—would not accept this new lifestyle immediately, but the old ones and the women would do the farming and
in time the new life would be accepted by all.

When nothing came of his request, Yellow Wolf repeated it the
following year to Thomas Fitzpatrick, then Cheyenne-Arapaho
agent, who merely scoffed. Instead of receiving a protective fort,
implements, seeds, and breeding stock, the Cheyenne received
bullets. In 1847, according to Berthrong, the Cheyenne chief Old
Tobacco tried to warn a government wagon train of the
Comanches' hostility. As he entered the camp, he was fired upon
and killed. The dying chief urged his family and friends not to
seek revenge, stating that his friends had not realized it was him
when they shot.

With the death of Old Tobacco, trouble truly began. Death's
sabbatical was over. Young Indian men, fired to the boiling point
on rotgut whiskey, stopped wagon trains heading west and
begged a little tobacco, a sack of coffee, a bolt of calico. This,
they reasoned, was not much to ask of the white men who
crossed their lands, felled their timber, and shot their buffalo,
leaving the bulk of his carcass to decay while the Indians starved
and died. But to the white people, these young men with painted faces and bows and arrows presented a fearsome sight. The
emigrants raised their guns and fired. A brave fell from his pony.
War cries sounded, the train was attacked, and many people
died. Troops were sent to punish the Indians. More gunfire was
exchanged, more lives lost. Retaliation brought more depreda-

tion, and blood bathed the plains.

In 1857, Yellow Wolf and his people were at Bent's Fort waiting peacefully for supplies when troops led by General Sumner arrived. They took what they wanted of the supplies and gave the rest to the Arapahoes. Seeing their women and children helpless and surrounded by troops, Yellow Wolf and some of the other chiefs decided to flee up beyond the North Platte, where people lived peacefully.

But trouble continued on the plains. The Colorado territory had become a hotbed. The wild and savage Indian was in the way of progress, of army careers, of white farmers and ranchers, of gold prospectors. Headlines in New York City, Boston, and Philadelphia newspapers screamed atrocities geared to excite the white population to encourage Washington to send more troops west to protect their relatives. And with more troops sent, more blood, Indian and white, was shed.

There were fewer and fewer Indians to replace those who were killed, but a seemingly endless line of whites: new European immigrants from the slums of bulging Eastern cities, illiterate itinerants, renegades, criminals, runaway slaves. Society's dropouts littered the army posts. It was hardly a case of controlling Indians but of exterminating them. Then, in 1861, the Civil War broke out. Reports reached Yellow Wolf that a new Great Father, Abraham Lincoln, sat in the white man's council and that whites were now killing their own brothers, fathers, and sons. Much of the army had been withdrawn from the west and sent east to fight for the Great Father. Even the endless streams of wagon trains had thinned along the Indian roads. Perhaps, Yellow Wolf reasoned, it was time to return to the adopted home on the Arkansas. William Bent would surely welcome them at the fort. The spirit of Old Tobacco called to him to make peace once more with the white brother. Nearing eighty, Yellow Wolf took up the pipe and with the chiefs to whom he had finally relinguished his power, counseled for the return. It was agreed that he, along with White Antelope, now nearly seventy-five, and his brother, Black Kettle, would lead their people south. They shared a hunger to see the Arkansas where so much of their lives had been spent and where the old ones had been dressed in ceremonial finery and placed upon scaffolds in the branches of cottonwoods growing at the river bank

Yellow Wolf's dream had not faded: once south, he would again approach the government with his plan to farm. With joy in their hearts, the Cheyenne slowly trekked south to visit relatives and the Bents and to reunite their lives with spirits of the old ones long passed into the world of shadows.

To the Cheyenne's surprise and dismay, they found not fewer whites but more in the old hunting grounds. Towns had sprung up with the discovery of gold in Colorado; army posts, trading posts, and stage coach way stations had been constructed. There was less game and more cattle grazing the plains; fewer berries and cottonwoods but more mounds of dirt in which whites lived like prairie dogs. The Great Father had not recalled all the pony soldiers. There was a small garrison at Fort Lyon, the fort William Bent built in 1859. Bent, grown older himself, had sold the new fort to the government as an army post, and he lived quietly on his ranch near the Purgatoire River. Nonetheless, the Cheyenne returned to their old haunts and were happy along the Arkansas.

But the confrontations continued. There were brutal murders committed, raids on ranches and way stations, and the roads were closed to both emigrants and supply trains. Denver, cut off from supplies, seethed with rage and called for Indian scalps. A voluntary command, under Colonel John M. Chivington, was formed to punish the Indians, and Lean Bear, as well as Big Wolf and his family, were massacred by Chivington's troops.

Then Chivington and John Evans, the new governor of the Colorado Territory, met in Denver with a party of peaceful chiefs who had traveled to the city under the protection of Major Edward Wynkoop, commander of Fort Lyon. Wynkoop not only lent a sympathetic ear to the Cheyenne but believed in the chiefs' desire and pledge for peace. He wanted to make peace between the two factions and to receive reassurance that the Cheyenne would be protected by the army from both the army and Chivington's volunteers. The Cheyenne offered all white captives in their village as a sign of peaceful intention. The Denver group did not guarantee peace to the chiefs, but told them to move their village away from Fort Lyon where, they said, the government could not vouch for their safety. They were to camp near Sand Creek, some miles north of the fort, and were to send their men out to hunt as the government could not then afford to feed such a large group. Simultaneously, Major Wynkoop's transfer was arranged by Chivington, and Major Scott J. Anthony, who had less sympathy for the Indians was given the assignment.

In the moon of the hard frost, Yellow Wolf's people pitched tipis on Sand Creek's banks. At dawn on the cold morning of November 29, 1864, Colonel John Milton Chivington, a former minister, led his troops in a surprise attack against the village. Old White Antelope was one of the first to fall. War Bonnet fell; One Eye, later proven a paid government spy, fell. Women and children were butchered at Black Kettle's feet as he held a white flag in his hands, an American flag raised above his lodge.

Yellow Wolf, his frightened people unable to help him escape from the rapid fire, fell. He died as his enemies' horses sprayed bloodied snow upon his torn and mutilated body.

With Yellow Wolf's death, wishes for peace and plans to farm died. Stanley Vestal in *The Old Santa Fe Trail* (Bantam Books, 1957) remarked that the trail from the north had "led only to the Indians' graves...the white man is more deadly to his friends than to his enemies." Black Kettle followed the well-worn moccasin path and fled north. In 1868, still yielding to Yellow Wolf's counsel, he led his remaining band to the Washita, the red rocks of Indian Territory below the Arkansas. Blanketing his shame, the horror of defeat and loss of human dignity, he kept his eyes on the trail of peace. William Bent, old and despondent and saddened to the heart for his people, the Cheyenne, joined Yellow Wolf in the land of the shadows in 1869.

THE MURDER OF JACK SMITH

John Simpson Smith, born in 1810 in Frankfort, Kentucky, had trekked west from St. Louis in 1830. He became a mountaineer, trapper, trader, scout and interpreter, and married a Cheyenne girl, Na-to-mah, who bore him a son, Jack. The first mention of Jack is found in the writings of Lewis H. Garrard. In 1846, Garrard, a young man of seventeen, made the trek over the Santa Fe Trail, eventually coming to Bent's Fort in Southeastern Colorado. There he became acquainted with John Smith, and at Smith's invitation went to live in Yellow Wolf's Cheyenne village, where he met Smith's Indian family. According to his journals from that time:

> Little Jack, three or four years of age, clung behind his mother, plainly showing in complexion and features the mingling of American and Indian blood. His grey eyes are continually centered on me, but I could say nothing intelligible to him, as he spoke only the Cheyenne tongue.

Garrard further described a domestic scene in the Indian village:

> Smith's son Jack took a crying fit one cold

night, much to the annoyance of four of five chiefs, who had come to our lodge to talk and smoke. In vain did the mother shake and scold him with the severest Cheyenne words, until Smith, provoked beyond endurance, took the squalling youngster in his hand; he "shu-ed" and shouted and swore, but Jack had gone too far to be easily pacified. He then sent for a bucket of water from the river, and poured cupful after cupful on Jack, who stamped and screamed, and bit, in his puny rage. Notwithstanding, the icy stream slowly descended until the bucket was empty, another was sent for, again and again the cup replenished and emptied on the blubbering youth. At last, exhausted with exertion and completely cooled down, he received the remaining water in silence and, with a few words of admonition, was delivered over to his mother, in whose arms he stifled his sobs, until his heartbreaking grief and cries were drowned in sleep. What a devilish mixture Indian and American blood is!

On a journey with the Smith family, Garrard again observed and recorded the interplay of mother, father, and son:

Jack took a crying fit while under way. His mother tried to quiet him gently; Smith endured, impatiently, the fuss for a half-hour; but Jack keeping it up, was taken from his mother, who looked daggers askance at her

unfeeling lord, and jammed into the "dray,"
where he blubbered, unheeded, for two hours.

In this account there appears to be little love in the mother for
the father, nor does there seem to be much love in the annoyed
father for his son. The picture of young Jack Smith is completed
when he recounts the story of Jack's names:

> Jack has three names: that of Jack, so called by
> the white, and two Indian names...Wo-pe-kon-
> ne and O-toz-vout-al, the former meaning
> "White Eyes"...a nickname...the latter, his prop-
> er title..."Buck Eyes."

Indians usually assigned names from the most characteristic
aspect of a person, and "White Eyes" clearly indicates an early
differentiation from the other children in the village, a nickname
that identifies grey-eyed Jack as a half-blood.

Jack grew and developed, running at his mother's side and at his
father's heel, trekking in winter and summer from Indian village
to village, and from one trading post to another, constantly eyed
by full bloods as a curiosity, and by whites as the offspring of a
heathen and a heretic "squawman." The boy grew to be rather
tall, but thin and gangling. His knife-cut features and good looks,
marred by smallpox, were rarely sullied by the crease of a smile.
His lithe frame took easily to the saddle, and he rode as well as
any full blood.

Jack traveled with his father to St. Louis, and it must have been
at this time that Smith sent him east and had him educated. He
apparently expected Jack to return and help civilize the Indians

and was surprised and disappointed when Jack took another course.

In 1857, John Simpson Smith and his fourteen year old son, Jack, were panning for gold on lands held by the Cheyenne-Arapaho tribes near present-day Denver. When the Colorado gold rush began in 1858, the gold rushers met Smith at the mouth of Cherry Creek. Smith, fluent in the Indian languages, proved to be a great asset. He assisted in the building of the first cabin in Denver City in 1858. When a town company was formed by the miners and settlers, John Smith was invited to join because it was believed that his involvment in the settling of Denver would help protect the white interests from the land's owners, the Arapahos. Stan Hoig wrote in *The Sand Creek Masacre* (University of Oklahoma Press, 1961) that:

> For a time, "Uncle John" Smith took part in the settlement of the new city in the wilderness but his encounter with civilization was short-lived, and he was reportedly run out of town for beating his Indian wife with a three-legged creepy because she had danced with the miners.

This is a remarkable assertion. In the early years of the west, many traders, frontiersmen, or army men beat their Indian wives for one offense or another. It is rare that a wife-beater is reported to be chased out of town. It is more plausible that Smith had been run out of town for more pragmatic reasons. As George Bent reported in his correspondence, "Young Jack is said to have staked the first pay dirt ever found in Colorado. He panned out $222 worth of dust in one day on the site of Denver.

In other words, a young Cheyenne half-blood had the possibility of staking a claim to land developing into the townsite of the future city of Denver. It is almost too convenient a coincidence that his father should be run out of town.

As word of the gold in Colorado spread, more whites arrived. But instead of passing into the mountains, as they had in the California gold rush of 1849, they built towns and settled down to stay. The Indians, who had no need for gold, continued to accept the emigrants, but as more and more arrived, the buffalo on which the tribes depended for their very survival were frightened off or killed. Denver city continued to grow, and troubles festered as the Indians, dispossessed, hungry, and angry, became restless and contemptuous of all that surrounded them. Then, in April of 1860, a group of white men visited an Arapaho camp near the town when the men were gone, raped some of the women, and stole some of the mules. Reprisals were threatened by Chief Left Hand. Commissioner of Indian Affairs A. B. Greenwood recognized that the only alternative to peaceful coexistence with the Indians was to exterminate them. This was not, he believed, an acceptable alternative, and he recommended that a new treaty be worked out.

The Cheyenne and Arapaho people were invited to Fort Wise to sign this treaty in February of 1861. Under the agreement, the Indians would relinquish their claims to all lands except a gameless, arid section of southeastern Colorado Territory, which was to serve as a reservation for them. In return, the United States agreed to protect the Indians on the reservation, to pay them the sum of $30,000 a year for fifteen years, and to provide them with the stock, tools, and buildings necessary for them to farm their lands. John Smith, who had reappeared with a new Indian wife, served as translator during the Fort Wise treaty meetings, and a postscript to the treaty awarded half-bloods Robert Bent and Jack Smith each 640 acres of choice land along the Arkansas Valley.

When the Civil War began that same spring, federal troops were recalled east. Those troops left in the west were thin in number, poorly equipped, and suffering from low morale. The summer of 1861 was hot and dry and the country became parched. The tribes, who had not received the provisions promised by the treaty, were hungry. Several thousand gathered around the fort, threatening its security. They were temporarily quieted by the dispersal of a few provisions, but the Treaty of Fort Wise was never truly honored.

Early in 1863, Indian troubles began to develop in the Colorado Territory. In May, word had been received that the Cheyenne and Arapaho tribes were holding a secret meeting with the Sioux north of Denver for the purpose of uniting and driving the white man from the country. The Indians made it known that they considered the treaty of Fort Wise a swindle. Black Kettle and White Antelope both denied signing it, and the Cheyennes refused to leave their hunting grounds and go to the reservation where there was no game. Skirmishes continued throughout 1863. Wagon trains were attacked and the roads closed to traffic. Denver was blocked. The Union not only needed the gold from Colorado's mines but it also feared an alliance between the Confederacy and the Indians.

Then in 1864, the Hungate family, who had been peaceful farmers, were brutally murdered. This atrocity was laid to Roman Nose, a Cheyenne, and the Dog Soldiers, the main warrior contingent. Their mutilated bodies were brought to Denver and displayed to the people, touching off panic, anger, and talk about reprisal. In June, John Evans, governor of the Colorado Territory, issued a proclamation which directed all friendly Indians to go to places of safety, where they were to be given provisions. The object of this, he said, was to prevent friendly Indians from being killed through mistake. The Cheyennes and Arapahoes from the Arkansas valley area were directed to report to Fort Lyon. Black Kettle and his people set up their camp about forty miles away on Sand Creek, where they were soon joined by other bands, two-thirds of which were women and children. The post commander, Major John Anthony, assured Black Kettle that they would all be safe there and told them to go out and hunt buffalo until such time as provisions could be acquired for them.

In Black Kettle's village at Sand Creek were the half-bloods Jack Smith, who held title to lands along the Arkansas River, and Charlie Bent. On the morning of November 29, 1864, the village was attacked by troops led by Colonel John M. Chivington. During the course of this infamous massacre, Smith and Bent were taken prisoner and placed for safekeeping under the surveillance of James Beckwith, the old trapper who helped guide the troops to Sand Creek, and Jack's father, John Smith. Charlie Bent, fifteen years old, held no title to land, nor had he panned gold in Cherry Creek. He had, however, led attacks against whites. Jack Smith had often been pegged a murderous renegade, but few accusers provided positive evidence of his alleged crimes. Jack had been sent back east to be educated, and his smattering of education in two cultures could and occasionally did play a large part in the Plains Indians' struggle to maintain their lands and a free, nomadic way of life. He could read the false documents presented to the Indians by the government, and he did have some influence with his white relatives. There were those eager to pin depredations on Jack, and there was a feeling of general aversion to him.

According to the Reports of the Committee, "The Chivington Massacre," United States Congress, Senate, 39th Congress, 2nd Session, Jack's father testified:

> As I was sitting inside the camp, a soldier came up outside and called me by name. I got up and went out, he took me by the arm and walked toward Colonel Chivington's camp, which was about sixty yards from my camp. Said he, "I'm sorry to tell you, but they are going to kill your son Jack." I knew the feeling toward the whole camp of Indians, and that there was no use to make any resistance. I said, "I can't help it." I then walked on toward where Colonel Chivington was standing by his campfire; when I got within a few feet of him, I heard a gun fired and saw a crowd run to my lodge, and they told me Jack was dead.

The identity of Jack's murderer or murderers was not established. With all the exacting detail brought to light in the subsequent investigations it appears odd that no one could name the killer. Indeed, some denied that there had been a murder. In a letter written to his brother, Major Anthony said, "We, of course, took no prisoners, except John Smith's son, and he was taken ill and died before morning." Major Hal Sayr stated that he thought Jack had accidentally killed himself while cleaning a gun. Another report stated that Jack was standing outside the lodge door talking with a soldier. This soldier held a carbine in his hands, cocked and pointed toward Smith. The gun went off, killing Smith immediately, and the soldier pretended it was accidental.

James Beckwith, who was in the lodge at the time of Jack's death, testified:

> He [Jack Smith] was sitting in the lodge with me...There was a piece of lodge cut out where the old man went out. There was a pistol fired through this opening and the bullet entered his [Jack Smith's] breast. He sprang forward and fell dead, and the lodge scattered, soldiers, squaws, and everything else. I went outside myself, as I went out I met a man with a pistol in his hand. He made this remark to me, 'I am afraid the damn son of a bitch is not dead.'...We took him out and laid him out of doors. I do not know what they did with him afterwards.

Some authors have claimed that Jack was a government spy, or a paid informer, or the guide who led the troops to Black Kettle's village. There is no evidence to suppport these claims, however, and Jack Smith remains today what he was in the middle 1800s: a half-blood with an education his father hoped would turn him from "savagry," a man whose reputation as a renegade and murderer was never substantiated. He is perhaps simply the victim of the enormous mistrust people who live in two worlds must bear from those of both worlds.

More likely, settlers and ranchers coveted the large tract of land along the Arkansas that he held title to, and it would have seemed an atrocity to allow a Cheyenne half-blood not only to have the reputation of having panned the first gold in Cherry Creek but to stake a claim on land appointed as the townsite of the future city of Denver. The gold strike alone would have been sufficient reason for murder.

The Sand Creek massacre led to a holocaust. Chivington lit a fire that burned across the western plains for nearly two decades. The results were not only the decimation of the Plains Indians but heavy suffering for the white population as well. After that cold November morning when Jack Smith was murdered, nearly all of the Indian tribes on the Plains exploded into violence. Thereafter, the Indian would no longer claim innocence as a "savage." The slain at Sand Creek, the half-blood among them, had their deaths avenged.

ROMAN NOSE, CHEYENNE: A BRIEF BIOGRAPHY

When, in the early 1830s, Cheyenne chief Yellow Wolf pointed out to the Bent brothers and Ceran St. Vrain the most advantageous location for their trading post, he, in a sense, opened his robes and those of his brothers of the southern plains to the teeth of progress, to manifest destiny.

Soon, along with the cottonwoods and the land, the buffalo began to disappear. Buffalo, to the plains Indians, was food, clothing, weapon, utensil, decoration and almost religion. From its back came the lodge and dress; from its bones came needles, awls, spoons, knives; from its guts came water bags and cooking pots; from its flesh came meat. Even the tail of the buffalo was used to swish off bothersome insects on hot, sticky days. Nothing was wasted. Everything was important, even its excretion, for that, having dried under the sun, could be burned for fuel. The buffalo came to be the coin of barter.

Also, the buffalo, *pte*, was considered the only animal worthy of sacred rites. Without *pte*, the Indian was doomed, and as the buffalo disappeared from the plains so, too, the Indian disappeared. The white man's gun did not defeat the Indian. It was the death of the buffalo which brought the Cheyenne, the Sioux (Lakota), the Arapaho, and other nations of the plains, to starvation and decline on reservation lands, those empty, sterile enclosures of stagnation and death.

Two Cheyennes prominent during the mid-1800s were Black Kettle and Roman Nose. The "peace chief" Black Kettle, who took up the pen and treatied land away, was considered a "good" Indian. Roman Nose, the fierce Dog Soldier warrior who took up the feathered lance and attempted to hold that land, was considered a "bad" Indian. Both men, thinking of their people, meant to preserve the old ways and to insure the survival of their race, their nation, their culture. In a sense, both fought bitterly to protect the Cheyenne way against a common enemy. Black Kettle, a statesman, hoped to preserve the way through diplomacy; Roman Nose, of a definite military nature, hoped to preserve the way through force. He would not compromise at council fires nor settle for a reservation and a vegetable garden.

Black Kettle, who had married into the *Witapiu* band of the south, hunted along the Arkansas River. Roman Nose, of the northern *Hmisis,* roamed along the Southern Platte and Smoky Hill Rivers, and often camped with the Sioux. The various Cheyenne bands came together once a year to perform the Sun Dance, and occasionally for the great and holy ceremony of renewing the Sacred Arrows. The peoples of the northern and southern bands intermarried regularly, which kept blood ties, war pledges and the language intact.

It was while roaming along the Platte in 1864 that Roman Nose learned of the Sand Creek Massacre and of how Black Kettle had raised both the American flag and a white flag as a sign of peace when the soldiers approached. He had been one of the few lucky enough to escape with his life. The news traveled swiftly. Roman Nose mourned the deaths of those "friendlies" and the misery of the survivors, but he had no use for chiefs who signed tribal lands away. Black Kettle was an old fool, he may have thought, and too old to have been leading the people. Ever the warrior, Roman Nose vowed that his lance and carbine would drive the white man from the plains.

Roman Nose managed to persuade and enlist many of the hot-headed young men of Black Kettle's *Witapiu* to join with him and the Dog Soldiers. They were also joined by Charlie and George Bent, both looking for blood and revenge after Colonel John M. Chivington's devastation at Sand Creek. Charlie and George, both half-bloods, had seen many of their blood relatives slaughtered. With a greatly enlarged and revitalized force, Roman Nose rode against the whites, mainly emigrant wagon trains and ranches. They were the enemy! It was the settler who destroyed the land and drove the buffalo off or left his unused carcass to rot in the sun. It was the settler and iron horse builder who brought the blood-thirsty, glory-hungry bluecoats into the land of the setting sun.

Roman Nose was labeled every conceivable epithet. He was acclaimed fierce, daring and brave. He was even called handsome and powerful. He was considered, after victories, a knowledgeable tactician. He was only rarely called human! He was infamous for ferocity, anger and the malicious murder of "innocent whites." Yet these "innocents" were stealing his earth and ripping it apart with plows; they were driving his brother, *pte*, off with fences and the iron horse. These "innocents" unleashed a plague of diseases upon his people: smallpox, cholera, tuberculosis, and the final sickness of whiskey. Not only were their bodies and minds weakened but the spirit had deafened to the call of "hookahey." The people were becoming weak-hearted children who sat about the tipi gossiping of a morning, sucking nipples of the white man's gifts: weevil infested flour, rotted beef, and watered whiskey.

Whiskey had become an extension of the lie told to the Indians by the white man. The chiefs had asked for guns and ammunition with which to hunt. They were given instead cheap glass beads, blankets that fell apart at the first washing, Civil War uniforms that let in the cold winter through every seam, and whiskey to drag the proud nation down into a desperate nation of drunkards. Women sold their horses for a bottle; men sold their land or their women.

After Sand Creek, Roman Nose reacted like any normal man wronged and deprived, swindled and cursed. It was either kill or be exterminated. His warriors would fight, restore the land and the game, and the natural dignity of a proud nation. He would lead the charge. Colonel Chivington slaughtered more than hostile savages at Sand Creek: he ultimately slew his own kind.

The exact place of Roman Nose's birth remains disputable, but he was born, probably, north of the Platte River near the Black Hills, *Paha Sapa,* around 1838-1839. He was first named Surt or Sauts, which translates into "the Bat," because of his daring swiftness, which made him difficult to kill or catch in battle. The cavalry, upon seeing him in profile in the theatre of war, called him "Roman Nose." The name stuck, and he adopted the sobriquet himself, taking the name Wogun Weguini, or Wo-o-khi-nih (Hooked Nose).

A member of the Elk Society, as a war leader of the Crooked Lances he rode with the renowned warriors Red Cloud of the Sioux and Dull Knife of the Cheyenne. But while Dull Knife made his reputation in warfare among Indians, Roman Nose made his against the whites. He married a cousin of Edmond Guerrier, brother-in-law of the younger Bent boys. Almost nothing is known of his father or other members of his immediate family. Only a footnote attests to a brother, Left Hand, who rode at his side in the Platte Bridge fight and died.

Roman Nose was a highly religious man. Wooden Leg recorded one example of this spirituality:

> ...once when we were camped on Goose Creek...the medicine water lake was not far away. At dawn, Roman Nose stripped himself, made a raft of logs and went out upon the lake. He took with him his medicine pipe. He had a large buffalo robe for a bed and a small one for a pillow. No food, no water for drinking. He spent the day on his robe. He prayed, "Great Medicine, let me conquer all enemies," and other prayers of this kind.

For four days he stayed upon the raft, the nights being frought with the dangers and perils of thunder, lightning, hail, and rain. All thought he would die.

> When the quiet light of morning came, two men went upon a hill to search over the waters. There was Roman Nose still floating on his raft. They helped him to land and to put himself upon the shore. Not a hailstone had hit him. The water spirits failed to devour him. The Great Medicine prevented them. At the camp, all of the old men sat themselves in a circle and listened to his rehearsal of the events of his great devotional adventures.

Physically, he was a powerful man, standing slightly better than six feet and weighing somewhere between 220 and 240 pounds. Big chested, strong limbed, he was handsome with fierce, piercing eyes set in a muscular face with heavy brows etched under a high forehead. He carried himself with easy confidence. When not in battle, he wore beaded buckskin leggings, a flannel shirt, a buffalo robe, and a single upright eagle feather in his black hair. In battle, he dressed in a cavalry soldier's blue jacket with shiny gold epaulettes, his famous war bonnet trailing the wind. He painted his face yellow over the forehead, red across his nose and black was smeared across the mouth and chin. Much has been made of the Indians' painting the body, but it was ceremonial and no more savage than his white brothers' propensity and enjoyment of color and decoration.

Roman Nose was described by one general as:

> A veritable man of war, the shock of battle and scenes of carnage and cruelty were as the breath of his nostrils; about thirty years of age, standing six feet three inches high, he towered, giant-like, above his companions. A grand head with strongly marked features, lighted by a pair of fierce black eyes, a large mouth with thin lips, through which gleamed rows of strong, white teeth; a Roman nose with dilated nostrils like those of a thoroughbred horse, first attracted wide attention, while a broad chest, with symmentral limbs on which the muscles under the bronze of his skin stood out like twisted wire, were some of the points of this splendid animal. Clad in buckskin leggings and moccasins elab-

orately embroidered with beads and feathers, with a single eagle-feather in his scalplock, and with the rarest of robes, a white buffalo, beautifully tanned and soft as cashmere, thrown over his naked shoulders, he stood forth, the war chief of the Cheyennes.

Although there is obvious admiration in this description, note the constant analogies to an animal. Roman Nose has been stripped of nearly all human qualities and stands like a thoroughbred on the block. It should also be noted here that the assertion that Roman Nose wore a white buffalo robe is in error. As George Bird Grinnell stated in *The Fighting Cheyennes* (University of Oklahoma Press, 1966), "Roman Nose never wore a white buffalo robe. To the Cheyenne the white buffalo was a sacred object, which might not be handled or used by anyone."

Roman Nose was courageous, a splendid fighter and esteemed by the entire Cheyenne nation. Many years after his death, Wooden Leg wrote:

Roman Nose was, I believe, the most admired of all warriors I ever saw. He was killed when I yet was a boy, but I remember him as an example for the young men...At various Great Medicine dances he went bravely through the bodily torture as a sacrifice of self for the good of the tribe.

His bravery came naturally and his influence was enormous as he was the acknowledged leader in war even though he was not a chief. He had refused a chieftancy (like Crazy Horse of the

70

Sioux) when young, on the grounds that he spent the major portion of his time in battle rather than in council. He had not been blessed with the gentle or paternal qualities usually ascribed to a civil chief. He knew that his easily fired emotions were suited for battle, not for councils.

His major battles and great victories were those of Fort Phil Kearney, Platte Bridge, Julesburg and Fort Wallace. George Bent described one of Roman Nose's more famous forays against the cavalry on the Powder River in September of 1865:

> Everyone noticed him as he came up on his pony. The Indians were in line. Cole's men were in line, one-half a mile long, from river to hill with cannon in centre of line. They were fighting (firing) shells at Indians behind us on hill. We were in line behind a lowhills [sic]; Roman Nose came up he said for all to get ready. He was going to ride up and down before the soldiers. (To draw off fire.) He then rode down towards river and started towards hill, riding whole length of the line with soldiers all shooting at him, and then the Indians charged. C's whole line was now in confusion as the Indians rode at it. When we were within a hundred yards they fired grape and killed several ponies, but no Indians.

Credit was also given to the warriors under Roman Nose after the battle of Beecher Island, due mainly to his strong leadership, although his forces suffered many dead and wounded. It was because of certain peculiarities of that battle that Roman Nose found a place in the pantheon of warriors.

He first became known to eastern America because of a confrontation with General Winfield Scott Hancock (called Old Man
of the Thunder by the Cheyenne) and George Armstrong Custer,
otherwise known to his troops as "Hard Backsides" or "Iron-ass
Curly." Hancock, supposedly bringing that ounce of prevention
to the plains in the winter-spring of 1866, was searching for
Indian scalps. Custer rode eagerly out to count coup on hostile
savages. It was his first time out on the plains and the first time
he was confronted with an Indian who did not face him from the
pages of James Fenimore Cooper's romantic novels.

Custer might have had a predilection for pretty Indian maidens, but he was an avowed hater of the male progenitor. Glory
hunter he might have been, but butcher he became. Custer, fresh
to the plains from the bloody fields of Civil War fame and glory,
may have thought he still chased Confederates when he marched
on Indians. Soldier to the polished brass, stout commander to
the brink, he was nonetheless foolheartedly, in love with his commission, his battalions, his dedication, and his decidedly ascend-
ing career. Vain, impetuous, possibly suffering psychological
damage, his image as the dashing cavalry officer of the famed
golden locks and buckskin uniform was the stuff of romance and
legend, which he encouraged. Though Custer claimed great
respect for the Indian and his free way of life, he held more com-
passion for his hunting dogs than for any nation of Indians.

Hancock had none of the saving graces possessed by Custer,
nor the excuse of being a young romantic. Custer was twenty-
seven when he took command of the 7th Cavalry on the Kansas
plains in 1866. Hancock was a grizzled veteran in the arts of per-
suasion and war. General Hancock was a fool, an aging soldier

with little time to grasp glory and less ingenuity with which to obtain it. Custer's hunger for adoration brought about his demise; the uncontrolled anger and frenzied paranoia of Hancock restricted his accomplishments. The Indian fought for survival, the cavalry officer often for decoration. Hancock's pomposity darkened his greatest moment, and his bruised dignity led him into disgrace and failure. In his blindness, he ordered a Cheyenne village burned and started a totally new war.

The Dog Soldiers, combined forces of Cheyenne, Sioux (Lakota) and Arapaho under the leadership of Tall Bull, Pawnee Killer and the military command of Roman Nose, had been raiding on the central plains and committing depredations upon emigrants, settlers, telegraph stations, railroad workmen and U.S. military posts. Hancock and Custer were in pursuit.

Hancock, through the strenuous efforts of two Indian agents, Jesse Leavenworth and Edward Wynkoop, forced a meeting with the chiefs of the Dog Soldiers. The General demanded the presence of Roman Nose and was furious that the warrior had evaded the council. He insisted upon a meeting. The valorous Cheyenne, surely flattered by Hancock's ignorance of the Cheyenne's civilian state, marched toward Hancock's camp with a scarlet sash about his waist, his gold epaulettes shining in the light, and a white flag of truce on the guidon in his hand.

Custer later described the coming together of the Indians and his troops:

> At 11 a.m. we resumed march, and had proceeded but a few miles when we witnessed one of the finest and most imposing military displays, prepared according to the Indian art of war, which it has ever been my lot to behold. It

was nothing more nor less than an Indian line of march; as if to say: thus far and no further. Most of the Indians were mounted; all were bedecked in their brightest colors, their heads crowned with the brilliant warbonnet, their lances bearing crimson pennants, bows strung, and quivers full of barbed arrows.

Then, according to George Bent, in his correspondence:

After a few moments of painful suspicion General Hancock, accompanied by General A.J. Smith and other officers, rode forward, and through an interpreter invited the chiefs to meet midway for the purpose of an interview. In, response to this invitation, Roman Nose, bearing a white flag, accompanied by Bull Bear, White Horse, Grey Beard, and Medicine Wolf on the part of the Cheyennes, and Pawnee Killer, Bad Wound, Tall Bear that Walks under the Ground, Left Hand, Little Bear and Little Bull on the part of the Sioux, rode forward to the middle of the open space between the two lines.

Three hundred painted warriors had stretched in a straight line for one mile across the open prairie, a tactical display worthy of a Roman general, and probably proposed by Roman Nose. We can only surmise how impressed Hancock, who commanded a superior number of forces, something like seven to one, must have been. Roman Nose had come to meet with the pony soldier chief, and, in military fashion, was determined to display his might. He was also determined to kill Hancock by his own hand, as George Bent wrote in a letter to George Hyde. In fear that his emotional temper would flare and erupt, thus endangering the lives and welfare of the helpless ones camped only a few miles off, he kept the calm Bull Bear at his side as a measure of restraint.

The two armies met on the exposed plains. Hancock crudely snapped at the war lord, and demanded to know whether the war leader of the Dog Soldiers desired peace or war. It was reported that Roman Nose sarcastically replied, "We don't want war. If we did we would not come so close to your big guns."

Hancock asked why he hadn't brought the entire vlllage with him then if war had not been planned. Roman Nose answered, "Are not women and children more timid than men? The Cheyenne warriors are not afraid but have you never heard of Sand Creek? Your soldiers look just like those who butchered the women and children there."

Hancock sputtered, but Tall Bull, standing next to Roman Nose, interjected:

> We never did the white man any harm. We don't intend to. We are willing to be friends of the white man...the buffalo are diminishing fast. The antelope, that were many a few years ago, they are now thin. When they shall all die we shall be hungry; we shall want something to eat, and we will be forced to come into your camp. Your young men must not fire at us; whenever they see us they fire, and we fire on them.

The Bull Bear also spoke:

> We have not been able to hold our women and
> children. They are frightened and have run
> away and they will not come back. They fear the
> soldiers.

Hancock, however, demanded the village move closer to his
camp. In that way only could he determine how powerful the
Dog Soldiers were.

Roman Nose responded, bitterly, that the weak ones had not
forgotten Sand Creek. All had run off at the first sight of the pony
soldiers and were hiding in the hills. Hancock demanded their
return and sent the warriors to round them up. The general waited
two days for the first sign of movement along the horizon of
morning. When he realized they weren't going to return, he
ordered a large command, including Wild Bill Hickock, Edmond
Guerrier, and Custer to ride out and bring the Indians back for
proper punishment.

But Custer was easily deluded. He found the village but with
empty tipis, each with a small fire but not much else. On entering a lodge, according to Custer himself, he found a halfbreed
little girl huddled in the darkness who had been raped by the
younger warriors and left behind. [Note: Others reported that the
girl had been raped by Custer's troops.] In yet another lodge he
found a blind old man, also left behind. The rest of the people
had gone into the hills. Under Hancock's orders, Custer burned
and destroyed the village. Custer showed no mercy on the village
or the Indian's possessions, though he claimed to mourn the loss
of such beautiful "primitive" artifacts. With his Delaware scouts,
he managed to put most of these objects to the torch. The rest

became war spoils.

According to Custer in his book, *My Life on the Plains,* they pursued the band:

> Here we found the Indians had called a halt, built fires, and cooked their breakfast. So rapidly had we gained upon them that the fires were burning freshly, and the departure of the Indians had been so abrupt that they left several ponies with their packs tied to trees. One of the packs belonged to a famous chief, Roman Nose, who was one of those who met us at the grand gathering just before we reached their village a few days before. One of our Delawares who made the capture was very proud of the success, and was soon seen ornamenting his headdress with the bright crimson feathers taken from the wardrobe of Roman Nose.

If Custer referred to the famous war bonnet of Roman Nose, then his published statement is disputable. Roman Nose was an extremely religious man. He spent endless hours in preparing his medicine, his mind and his spirit. It is doubtful that even under duress he would neglect his war bonnet, which held such high religious significance. The bonnet had been made for him by the Cheyenne Medicine Doctor, White Bull, who was famous for his powers of creating medicine that protected warriors from soldiers' bullets. Occasionally called "Ice" because of his power to eject ice from his mouth during sacred ceremonies, White Bull had used his bullet-proofing powers successfully. The fierce Elk Society Leader approached White Bull to have him make a war-bonnet possessing those bullet-proofing powers, and Roman Nose was made a beautiful headdress. The story of how it came to be made, of two of the taboos connected with it, and of its various protective influences, was told to Wooden Leg by White Bull himself:

On one occasion during a storm, when it was raining and thundering, White Bull looked up into the sky and had a vision of a person there on horseback wearing a war-bonnet such as this, and by the side of this person was a hawk carrying in its feet a gun and a sabre. The thunder instructed White Bull to make a war-bonnet like the one he had seen, but it was not until long after this vision that he did so.

Once, however, when it was thundering, Roman Nose spoke to White Bull and asked him, "Do you ever see anything that will protect from lightning?" White Bull replied, "Yes, once I saw something." Roman Nose continued: "I once saw something too. Make that for me."

When making this warbonnet, White Bull first prepared a paint. He pounded to a powder many different colored stones, certain metals, black and yellow, yellow earth, some of the grass and other plants that sometimes came down from above, apparently frozen in the hailstones, as well as the powdered stone bones of great animals. The powder was mixed with clay. Before dressing, i.e. painting, black paint must be used, made of charcoal from a tree which had been set on fire by lightning, and yellow earth must be put on the body in spots, like hail. In front of the war-bonnet, close to the brow-band, and over the warrior's forehead, stood a single buffalo horn. Immediately behind this horn, on top of the bonnet, was the skin of a kingfisher, tied to the hair. At the right side of the head was tied a hawkskin. This hawk represented the person who in White Bull's vision had held in its claws the gun and the sabre. From the headpiece, on either side, two tails of eagle feathers ran down toward the ground, the feathers on the right side being red, and those on the left side white. At the back of the head, part way down on the war-bonnet, was the skin of a barnswallow, while to the right side of the warbonnet, where the feathers were red, was tied a bat, so that the warrior might safely fight in the night, for a bat flies at night and cannot be caught. The bat flies high-up, and you may throw things at him, but you will not hit him. Sometimes he will fly down, pursuing what is thrown at him. In a battle an enemy may shoot at the person who is wearing the charm but the one at whom he shoots is not really there in the flesh, as he appears to be: the real person is up above the bat. The swallow often flies close to the ground, working back and forth. The enemy may be shooting at the person on horseback, but what he is shooting at is not actually the person: the real person is the swallow, down below, flying close to the ground. The kingfisher which is tied to the head behind the horn was worn for the purpose of closing up holes which might be made in the body by bullets, because when the kingfisher dives into water, the water at once closes over it. When the bonnet had been prepared, and was to be given to Roman Nose, White Bull warned him, saying "After I have finished this and you put it on your head, you must never shake hands with anyone. If you do so, you will certainly be killed. If you get into any fight, try to imitate the call of the bird you wear on your head—the kingfisher." Besides this, one of the laws of the war-bonnet was like a law of the Contraries—that the wearer might not eat food that had been taken from a dish with a metal implement.

The man who wore this war-bonnet must have his horse dressed, i.e. painted, in a particular way. First a large scalp was tied to the horse's jaw, and zigzag lines, representing lightning were drawn down the front of the horse's legs. To paint a white horse, blue earth was used for these lines; for a black horse or a bay, white earth was used. A cream-colored horse, with white mane and tail, would have no lightning marks on his forelegs, but on both shoulders and both hips rainbows must be painted, four rainbows in all. Roman Nose had entire faith in this war-bonnet, and it was believed that it had

> always protected him in battle. He had worn it
> in many fights, especially in the year 1865,
> when on several occasions he rode back and
> forth within twenty-five or thirty yards of lines
> of white troops, all of whom shot at him with-
> out effect...it is believed that he was killed
> because he unwittingly violated one of the laws
> of the war-bonnet

Quite obviously, Roman Nose would not leave his most powerful and important medicine behind for Custer's scouts to dance over. Custer either fabricated the story of the headdress or he was in error as to its ownership.

After Hancock gave the order to destroy the village, Roman Nose was more determined than ever to kill the general, but the warrior and his band fled south to Black Kettle's village. Furious and frustrated, Hancock returned to Fort Hays, Kansas, and, in prompt time, to the East. His forays had led nowhere but to disgrace. The hostiles were more vehement than ever and the depredations spread across the plains with fiery vengeance.

In 1867 Washington planned a great council with the warring bands of the Southern plains, the Medicine Lodge Creek Council. Hostile Kiowa, Comanche, Apache, Arapaho and Cheyenne were called to parley their lands in exchange for a few wagons of, for the most part, useless gifts. Black Kettle brought his *Witapius* and camped south of the stream, a healthy distance from the soldiers. He remembered Sand Creek. There were those who still bore the scars of Chivington's guns and knives.

Once the hostile tribes had gathered, General William T. Sherman, the military commander of the Missouri Department, asked where the famous Dog Soldiers, and their equally famous leader, Roman Nose, were. The wary Cheyenne had received word that Sherman would be at Medicine Lodge Creek; Roman Nose purposefully stayed away because he was not a chief. Under Indian law, he had no authority to either speak nor touch the pen for the people. Government, and its various branches, never accepted the fact that a ferocious warrior might not be the civil head of a nation.

The council was delayed when Sherman was called to Washington on an emergeney. With Sherman gone, Roman Nose made his entrance at the council, creating a colorful, flamboyant display upon arrival. Marching four abreast, cavalry formation, his braves entered the vicinity; first at a soldierly walk, slowly working the piebald ponies to a trot, then canter, and at last a gallop. Whooping and firing guns in a grand parade of heroism and pride, the Dog Soldiers stormed the council grounds. The visiting official dignitaries, though warned beforehand of the peaceful procession, retreated in sheer fright for their scalps, as Roman Nose, the brilliant war-bonnet flaring behind, drew to a full stop at the edge of the council lodge. The display of Indian invention was beautifully staged—more likely than not by Roman Nose, who seemed to have a talent for theatrical spectaculars.

Major Edward Wynkoop, now the Cheyenne agent, arrived with young George and Charlie Bent acting as paid interpreters and runners. Indian anger rumbled across the summer on into autumn. Uneasiness stirred through the camps during September and October. Delays prompted fear and unrest. Tempers erupted. Black Kettle's life was threatened and that of his herd. The old sachem's power was on the wane. The young men would not listen to his counsel. Finally, all was ready, and chief followed chief to sign the treaty. Naturally the fine print was not read to the Indians. Even Bent and Smith somewhat failed their Indian brothers. Wynkoop, also a trusted friend, might have offered a warning, but he held back. The chiefs touched the pen to a deceitful lie. They signed their lands away. The tribes were to hunt thereafter below the Arkansas River in Indian Territory, Oklahoma.

On hearing the details, Roman Nose flared in anger. He was never to hunt the Smoky Hill River region again. Those ancient lands had been assigned to the whites, and they would build trails for the iron horse. The construction of the railroad had been halted due to Indian depredations and the Treaty Council was called mainly to insure the safety of its completion. The link between east and west coasts must be soldered to the point of genocide. Nothing must impede manifest destiny.

Roman Nose must have raised his eyes to the Great Spirit of the Universe, and hurled his lance into the earth with such force that thunder rolled in the bowels of the earth. These were his lands by birthright. Nothing could deny nor negate this right. These were his people's hunting grounds. The peace chiefs who had touched the pen for a wagon of junk had no power over his existence. In the falling light of dusk, Roman Nose and his Dog Soldiers, commanded by Tall Bull, slipped from the council and left their unwanted presents behind, never again to parley with the white man. Roman Nose was one of the few important Indian leaders never to touch pen to a Washington treaty.

The buffalo were still somewhere on those vast plains. Wogun Woguini, Hooked Nose, would be there to hunt with his brother, to pray for his survival, or, if he must, to fall beside him in extinction under the bluecoats' fire. That was the Cheyenne way. Yellow Wolf had advised the people to put down the gun and scalp knife and take up the hammer and the plow, to trail the white man's cattle and drop seeds into the earth. He had been slaughtered at Sand Creek. Roman Nose had no intention of planting vegetables in a reservation garden.

In the summer of 1868, Major George (Sandy) A. Forsyth asked and received permission from General Phil Sheridan to outfit a fighting troop of men who had dealt for years in frontier warfare. Forsyth collected fifty men and one commissioned officer, Lieutenant Frederick H. Beecher, to assist him as second in command. The fifty men who comprised Forsyth's little army may have once been of the finest order, but they were recruited from the hell-holes of the west: drunks and thieves, out of work buffalo hunters, war veterans without a battalion, burnt-out settlers, and Indian haters. They welcomed the opportunity to feast on army rations of beans and coffee. Dressed in buckskins and armed with knives, Spencer six-shooters, and a flask or two of whiskey, these veterans rode out with Major Forsyth to combat the warring bands of Pawnee Killer and Roman Nose. The alliance of Sioux, Cheyenne and Arapaho were equally hot in pursuit of whites. They were determined to drive them from the Smoky Hill River area.

The Indian alliance, having discovered Forsythe's troops, celebrated with a feast the night before the planned attack. Roman Nose was invited to take food in the lodge of a Sioux chief. The war pipe was passed around the circle. It was first offered to the four cardinal points of the universe, and then to the all above and the all below. A pinch of the earthen floor was taken up and blown across the shadows of the lodge. The pipe was passed again and again. There would be victory in the morning. Roman Nose would lead the first charge, and all knew that he could not be killed by the soldiers' bullets when wearing his famed war bonnet. At the side of the fire, in the place reserved for guest of honor, Roman Nose enjoyed the company of host and friends. He laughed quietly and joked with those around him.

On this eve in the Moon When the Deer Paw the Earth, he was filled with the power of confidence instilled by his war bonnet. He was neither smug nor vain. He had the intelligence not to rely totally upon this protection, and knew through experience that the fighting power of his braves would determine the outcome of the battle. His medicine would not insure success; it would only protect him in the flare of battle. He spoke calmly and intelligently to the gathered headmen that they must fight like the bluecoats, together in line, constantly astride the ponies, not skirmish or fight as snipers from behind rocks or a hill. They would charge directly upon the enemy, overwhelming the soldiers with strength of their powerful forces. Were there not some six hundred warriors and merely fifty white men with two additional officers in uniform! This would be like hunting a single rabbit if the warriors fought together as a body, not running wild as though crazy with the white man's whiskey. During the night, he outlined his plans and strategy. Everyone listened carefully and envisioned the dawn attack.

The Sioux women brought food which had been cooked in an adjoining tipi. Dog meat and buffalo were passed to hungry warriors. Fried bread, a delicacy, was brought and heavily sweetened coffee was poured. The warriors ate ravenously, for who knew, it might be their last chance to eat for some time, or it might be the last time they ever ate.

Roman Nose observed the manners and protocol of the lodge. He ate with his fingers, sucking them dry of any morsel stuck to them. He ripped apart the fried bread and bit into the steaming flesh. It was good, and he enjoyed the meal with relish, passing compliments to his host and the women who had prepared the feast. He ate quickly for he intended to get to sleep early.

Again the pipe was passed and the leading men of the three bands, an alliance as strong as the rocks of *Paha Sapa,* flattered each others' prowess and retold tales of valor and victory. Roman Nose squatted in the shadows, not wishing to glorify himself. Nonetheless, he took pleasure from hearing the accounts of his friends' bravery. As he silently passed the pipe to the warrior at his right, Eight Horns, a young Dog Soldier, entered the lodge. The young man circled behind the chiefs and halted beside Roman Nose, who calmly listened to his whispers. Startled, he pitched forward, his head nearly touching the floor of the lodge. As he rose, a loud noise, as if from great pain, slipped through his parted teeth. He stood and announced that he would go to his lodge. A great disaster had occurred. He would not take part in the dawn battle. As he left with White Bull, Eight Horns spoke to the council. Roman Nose, unknowingly, had eaten food touched by iron. The fried bread, that he had broken apart and eaten with such enjoyment, had been lifted from the splattering grease by an iron fork. His medicine was broken. The celebrants disbanded in great consternation.

Before the pearl light of dawn rimmed the horizon, another misfortune occurred. A group of eight young braves, eager for honors, stole off from the village and had attacked Forsyth's command by running off seven horses. Now Forsyth's patrol knew that hostiles were in the direct vicinity. The Major ordered his troops to prepare for battle.

During the night, Roman Nose, with the aid of White Bull, began the long purification rites. White Bull advised that he would need many days to erase this bad medicine. He would need to go into the sweat lodge. All through the night, the warrior and shaman offered prayers to the Great Spirit, to the lightning, thunder, rain and hail. Prayers were given to the mother earth, and to the four points with the all above and the all below. When the sun rose high enough to spread its warm beams across the low bluffs of the flat lands, Roman Nose left his lodge and seated himself on a slight knoll in the direct light of the purifying sun. He closed his eyes and leaned back, hoping the heat of the sun would swirl his brain into spasms of dizziness which might bring about a vision suggesting a remedy for the blow fate had dealt. Time passed quickly. He knew others were already in battle, perhaps falling to the earth like the thud of raindrops.

At midday a group of warriors sought Roman Nose, and complained bitterly of their losses. They had driven the whites to an island in the center of the thin stream but could not rout them out. Unbeknownst to the Indians, two of the soldiers, young Jack Stillwell and Pete Trudeau, were hidden as snipers on the shore, concealed by the long grasses. On the island, under the protection of thick growth, plum trees and cottonwood saplings, and behind the barricades of their dead horses, the whites offered a battery of fire that struck and killed, or wounded, many Arapaho and Cheyenne. Dry Throat was dead. White Weasel Bear had been killed. Others were shot and wounded, perhaps mortally such brave warriors as White Thunder, son of White Horse, also Good Bear and Little Man of the Arapaho. They asked Roman Nose to come and lead the braves in the next charge.

Slowly, cautiously, painfully Roman Nose spoke. Once again, suffering, he reminded them that his medicine, his power had been broken.

> Something was done that I was told must not be
> done. The bread I ate was taken out of the frying pan with something made of iron. I have

been told not to eat anything so treated. This is what keeps me from making a charge. If I go into this fight, I shall certainly be killed.

Moments later, White Contrary arrived. He looked petulantly at old White Bull, whose medicine had obviously failed the war leader. Perhaps all his potions and frenzied prayers would fail. He dismissed the shaman with rudeness, and in disgust, White Contrary turned on Roman Nose and allowed his taunts to fly like barbed arrows.

White Contrary said that the people felt they belonged to him, to his leadership. But here he was between the hills sunning his face. What kind of man, what kind of warrior or leader was he, that would let his people down, people who had the utmost faith that he, Roman Nose, would lead their warriors to victory and drive the white man back from the Smoky Hill River to his villages by the sea of the rising sun.

The war leader responded with the story of the iron fork. White Contrary merely scoffed and replied that the people would only follow Roman Nose in this new way of fighting: in a line like pony soldiers. The people wanted him to show them how to strike these invaders from their land

Roman Nose rose and faced the mocking brave. He knew if he went into battle that day he would be killed. Knowing he would die, he called for his chestnut pony, mounted, and, kicking his heels into its flanks, rode off with White Bull beside him. At the lodge he prepared himself for battle. First he put on the bluecoat jacket with the gold epaulettes; he wound his crimson silk sash about his waist; he pulled on his beaded leggings and pushed his brown feet into new moccasins. Taking out a small hand mirror, he stared at the reflection. Tiredness and a wedge of fear showed at the corners of the small fierce eyes. He brushed a flame of yellow across his prominent brow, and stared once more into the mirror. He brushed a wide streak of vermilion across the famed hooked nose, and daubing into another pot of paints, brushed the black of victory across his mouth and determined chin. "Hookahey," he called, and lifted the beautiful war bonnet from his cherished medicine bundle. Shaking out the headdress in the brilliant light of the afternoon, he carefully inspected the kingfisher, the bat and the hawk feathers. Respectfully, almost lovingly, he placed the bonnet upon the crown of his head and tied the strings below the blackened chin. Once again he stared into the hand mirror, and then quickly mounted the chestnut pony and called out to the Great Spirit that it was a good day to die. "Nothing lives long but the earth and the mountains."

When old White Bull mounted his horse and rode out beside the brave leader, the younger man advised him to return to the village with the women and helpless ones. White Bull the great medicine man refused and trotted his horse onward, the flanks of the animal scraping those of Roman Nose's chestnut. White Bull would die today, too, thought Roman Nose, because of an iron fork.

A few women and children came out to watch the warriors take the victory now that Roman Nose was to lead the next charge. They stood, prominently exposed on the low bluffs above the river, well in sight of both their warriors and the white troop below. They sang strong-heart songs to their brave men and waved both Roman Nose and White Bull on to battle. The scrawny old medicine man, withered like drying grass, would not die beside his friend and prodigy. His life would not flutter away like a thin leaf of the plum tree that dropped in the swish of an arrow above the heads of the white troop. Roman Nose convinced the old medicine man to turn his pony.

A great shout rang out from the warriors. Two Crows announced Roman Nose had come to the line. White Contrary allowed a stiff smile to form on his lips. Roman Nose raised his lance and his carbine. His long shadow fell down from the slanting bluff upon grass and sand. By then it was late afternoon.

This time, in this battle, he would not ride out and circle round and round before the whites, drawing off fire, splashing dirt in their faces. He would call charge, and the warriors would divide and gallop along both sides of the fortress-island and then overrun the men firing from behind the breastwork of the dead horses.

Roman Nose called "hookahey" and the warriors charged, shouting their war songs and singing their death chants. They drew fire from the barricaded troops and two snipers hidden in the tall grasses on the mainland. Determination sent them back to the front lines of the charge. Braves fell; whites died also. Forsyth himself was hit and wounded in three places, and his aid, Lt. Beecher, and his surgeon were killed.

Roman Nose waved his carbine and charged. His chestnut splashed into the stream. Water sprayed and struck his exposed flesh. The horse stumbled to the river bank, stomping sand and grass, and suddenly trotted off, freed of its burden. Roman Nose had been hit. The bullet struck his back and ripped open his stomach. He had been shot by the snipers in the tall grass. He fell at the edge of the plum bushes and crawled under for cover. One of the snipers, probably Jack Stillwell, had made a direct hit.

The women on the bluff had witnessed the charge and the fall. Their screams of wailing for their fallen leader pierced the late afternoon and rose above the noise of the firing rifles.

The battle continued until nearly dark. Then the hush of quiet fell, with only spasmodic firing from the Indians to rip the night. Under the cover of darkness, in the descending shadows of the brilliant sunset, parties were sent out to retrieve the bodies of Roman Nose and the other braves who had been struck down. The entire village mourned. Many braves had fallen. The women gashed their arms and legs with the jagged edges of sharp stones, and they pulled out or cut their long hair. The suffering was great; their losses were greater.

A rumor circled the camp that Roman Nose had returned, that he had hidden in the tall grass and the plum bushes until light had lowered, and then crawled on his belly into the camp. It was also said that scouts found him and brought him back. However, he was in his lodge. Two Crows, Pawnee Killer, and White Bull, were with him. White Contrary and others stood near with the wife of the fallen warrior.

A series of wails rose from the encampment, and more people gathered at the entrance of the war lord's lodge. Two Crows left Roman Nose's side and went out to the people. Roman Nose would die, he told them. The young man, who was only in his late twenties, had lost all will to live. He had been shot through the back and spine. Were he to live, he would never stand again. A brave would rather die. White Bull came from the lodge and spoke briefly with Two Crows, who in turn announced that Roman Nose was dead.

The next morning his ponies and all his possessions were taken to the center of the village and left for whoever cared to take them away. The burial ceremony was solemnly performed, and Roman Nose's corpse, shrouded in a buffalo robe, was hidden on a platform entangled in the boughs of a cottonwood.

In November of that same year, Black Kettle's village, peacefully encamped on the Washita River in Indian Territory, was destroyed and the chief killed by the battalions of George Armstrong Custer.

The "good" and "bad" Indian had met the same fate, by the same hand: Manifest Destiny.

FORWARD

NATIVE AMERICAN ORAL TRADITION

In an unbroken continuum, the oral tradition reaches down to our day. Medicine people, elders, singers, poets, storytellers, and even children carry this strong commitment, this obligation, to ensure the longevity of the oral tradition. Among them are such native people as Leslie Marmon Silko, Joy Harjo, and Peter Blue Cloud. I, myself, sing the poem. It is a song not far from prayer, often in vocables—sounds without equivalent meanings, sounds which have untranslatable meanings, but sounds felt and understood by the traditional Native American participating listener.

This orality is the true, the pure lyric. It is not for the eye; it must be seen with the ear, heard in the heart, felt in the spirit. It is not necessarily intellectual, but it is rich in meaning and idea; the *adowe*, thanks to the creator for life and to all the creations for the gifts of food, water, habitat, clothing, light, etc. This emotion, or passion, is often mesmerizing. It can have healing properties. However, that is not to say that because you are a poet or a singer you are also a healer or medicine person.

The poet studies metrics, images, metaphor, cadence; the healer studies herbs, ointments, prayer, the flight of the hawk, the coil of the snake, the blush of the berry, the very essence of the spirit. Both may be visionaries, revealing vision through the oral chant.

The chant is part of a glorious, cleansing ceremony. It differs only slightly from the high Roman Catholic Mass, which traditionally contained prayer, song, its own particular *adowe,* and was conducted by what could be a healer, known as a priest.

There is nothing more stirring than an oral poem or prayer, especially when it is accompanied by a water drum and the sound of a hundred or more feet dancing, touching earth, the mother of us all; exciting the participatory listener to near frenzy, then further to a visionary state of being.

For the most part, the Anglo world, the non-Indian, non-tribal world, has lost its sense of tribalism and will probably never regain that communicative and spiritual experience, which indeed is shameful, tragic. Cultural roots must be respected, guarded, and practiced or the contemporary lifestyle will cloud and destroy this primal awareness, these sensations that touch the essences of life. Feet that have been shod do not touch the earth. Contemporary Indian roots are deep, but too many Native Americans, their feet shod, no longer touch earth, either, allowing the root to dry and turn to dust. And without roots, humankind is nothing.

WHITMAN'S INDIFFERENCE TO INDIANS

In vision and language Walt Whitman is America's Homer. His hero, however, was not the Greek classic—the noble individual of high birth—but the cumulative average. Bulk vastness and superlatives of "great" and "greatness" were his guidons. He was certainly a democratic nationalist, a flag waver. He was the poet of the ordinary person: butcher, baker, candlestick maker—but not of the Indian chief. He sang of the bus driver, the factory hand, the mechanic, the farmer, the ferryman of Brooklyn—but not of the feathered warrior.

Whitman sang electrically of nature; he created poems of the industrial boom in America and its dynamics, which thrust the nation into world leadership, secure in might and wealth but diseased with guilt. Everything which was American found a phrase in his verse, even the "common street prostitute."

Whitman wrote profusely of the woodcutter, the sailor, the frontiersman, the pioneer, the emigrant, generals such as Grant and Sheridan and Custer, and the army recruit, green and raw, courageous and wounded, stammering in his European accent in the new land of opportunity, sent West to protect the bulging population which was a target for feathered arrows.

Whitman's common man became the common soldier decidedly happy with "beans and hay." He became Whitman's noble man, embraced and paeaned for both his endurance and inherent stupidity. A job was a job—and killing Indians was a job, and jobs could not be found in the large eastern cities. He rigorously served under his new flag, and Whitman prodded him to glory. Everything which fell under Whitman's ken moved his poetic spirit: the lightning of the new skies and new horizons; the death of presidents; Denver, "queen city of the plains"; the "common earth, the soil"; William Cullen Bryant; the Battle of Gettysburg; Niagara Falls. He wrote America and America was his true hero, his Ulysses.

Everything America produced or which produced America was allowed a pentameter in Whitman's work—but only rarely the American Indian, the indigenous native to the land, what the Native American sons and daughters know as Mother Earth.

And yet Whitman was truly fascinated with Indian words and names and copied out many within an essay entitled "Slang in America": "Miss Bremer found among the aborigines the following names: Men's Horn-point; Round-Wind; Stand-and look-out; The Cloud-that-goes-aside; Iron-toe, Seek-the-sun; Iron-flash..." It is certainly understandable that anyone, especially such an imaginative and enthusiastic poet as Whitman, would find these names fascinating, but why as "slang"? How do they differ from John the Baptist or Richard the Lion-Hearted? As with these two English equivalents, the names pointed out particular characteristics of the person's nature, prowess, or accomplishments, obviously a fact Whitman failed to recognize.

Whitman gained employment as a minor clerk in 1865 in the Indian Bureau of the Interior Department in Washington, D.C. This employment was of short duration. He was soon dismissed by his puritan superior, James Harlan, who recoiled from the purloined pages of *Leaves of Grass*. Harlan believed the book was indecent and fired the "good gray poet." It would be expected that while Whitman was employed in this office he would have become acquainted with, and acutely aware of, the federal government's calculated plan to exterminate the Indians. The worthless treaties were at his fingertips; the recorded injustices perpetrated upon Indians were under his naked eyes; documents and letters of unscrupulous officials prodding the extermination of the "savages" most certainly would have been familiar to him. The horrifying slaughter of innocent Cheyenne and Arapahoe women and children at the infamous Sand Creek Massacre occurred only the preceding November of the year he took this employment. As many eastern liberals were greatly distressed by this mass murder, how was it that Whitman ignored those death cries? In the essay "An Indian Bureau Reminiscence," he wrote most clearly of his tenure there:

> After the close of the Secession War in 1865, I work'd several months (until Mr. Harlan turn'd me out for having written *Leaves of Grass*) in the Interior Department at Washington, in the Indian bureau. Along this time there came to see their Great Father an unusual number of aboriginal visitors, delegations for treaties, settlement of lands, &c.—some young or middle-aged, but mainly old men, from the West, North, and occasionally from the South—parties of from five to twenty each—the most wonderful proofs of what Nature can produce, (the survival of the fittest, no doubt—all the frailer examples dropt, sorted out by death)—as if to

show the earth and woods, the attrition of storms and elements, and the exigencies of life at first hand, can train and fashion men, indeed *chiefs,* in heroic massiveness, imperturbability, muscle, and that last and highest beauty consisting of strength—the full exploitation and fruitage of a human identity, not from the culmination-points of "culture" and artificial civilization, but tallying our race, as it were, with giant, vital, gnarl'd, enduring trees, or monoliths of separate hardiest rocks, and humanity holding its own with the best of the said trees or rocks, and outdoing them....

Let me give a running account of what I see and hear through one of these conference collections at the Indian Bureau, going back to the present tense.

Herewith he describes certain chiefs and their "outfits," which certainly take his eye's attention.

Let us note this young chief. For all his paint, "Hole-in-theDay" is a handsome Indian, mild and calm, dress'd in drab buckskin leggings, dark gray surtout, and a soft black hat. His costume will bear full observation, and even fashion would accept him. His apparel is worn loose and skant enough to show his superb physique, especially in neck, chest, and legs.

This sounds as if he's attempting to describe a horse on the block.

The descriptive catalog continues:

> Though some of the young fellows were, as I
> have said, magnificent and beautiful animals, I
> think the palm of unique picturesqueness, in
> body, limb, physiognomy, etc., was borne by the
> old or elderly chiefs, and the wise men.

This shockingly insensitive running account utterly fails to see a
single human quality other than a sensuousness in these men,
young or old, who had traveled far to the Capitol to bargain for
their lives, lands, liberty, culture, and survival with the "Great
Father." How could this alleged democratic humanitarian look
only at the "loose and scant" attire and discover merely the flesh
of these "magnificent and beautiful animals" without some sense
of shame for his connotative observation? He did not describe
the young recruit or his superior officers in such terms, in such
sensuous language. But then the recruit and Grant and Custer
were not animals, nor had they survived as the fittest by their
own natural wiles but by selective breeding and the slaughtering
wars, wars that raged across Europe for hundreds of years not so
much for the "survival of the fittest" but for the spoils those wars
offered. Whitman failed to see the lines of suffering and anxiety
in the faces of these men; he failed to hear their quick heartbeats;
he failed to feel any emotion with the exception of a hedonistic
fancy or possible appetite. But his estimate hardly differed from
that of his contemporaries. Even General George Custer admired
the physiques and prowess of these "beautiful animals." For the
larger part of his own creative life, Whitman was considered by
both society and most of the literati as a "criminal monster," an

outlaw of sorts. How is it he did not recognize kindred spirits — his counterparts in the Indian chiefs, warriors, or "wise men" who were also labeled "criminal monsters"? In another essay, "Some Diary Notes at Random," he described a ninety-four-year-old black slave he had known as a young boy in Long Island as "cute." Whitman claimed later in life to be an abolitionist.

In 1879 Whitman traveled west into southeastern Colorado to Fort Lyon, a mere horse ride from the site of the Sand Creek Massacre. Writing of his trip to Fort Lyon in *Specimen Days*, he fails to record that infamous slaughter:

> Between Pueblo and Bent's fort, southward, in a clear afternoon sun-spell I catch exceptionally good glimpses of the Spanish peaks. We are in southeastern Colorado—pass immense herds of cattle as our first-class locomotive rushes us along. We pass Fort Lyon—lots of adobe houses, limitless pasturage, appropriately fleck'd with those herds of cattle...a belated cowboy with some unruly member of his herd—an emigrant wagon toiling yet a little further, the horse slow and tired—two men, apparently father and son, jogging along on foot—and around all the indescribable chiaroscuro and sentiment (profounder than anything at sea) athwart these endless wilds.

No sign of a village of tipis, no buffalo in his sight, no plumed warrior, no woman tending child, no elder instructing youth and certainly no bloody massacre grounds, which were a fistful of miles away from his locomotive window. His published works contain not a whisper or suspicion of sympathy for those so brutally murdered and mutilated, including women and children, so that one day those immense herds of cattle might fleck that sea of grass at such places as the Chivington Ranch, located in slight approximation to his "first-class locomotive."

Although such silence about their fate might indicate his acquiescence in the planned extermination of all Indians in the Americas, Whitman does on occasion describe the red "savage" in a heightened understanding of, at least, the costume:

> Their feathers, paint—even the empty buffalo skull—did not, to say the least, seem any more ludicrous to me than many of the fashions I have seen in civilized society. I should not apply the word savage (at any rate, in the usual sense) as a leading word in the description of those great aboriginal specimens, of whom I certainly saw many of the best.

What he gives with one hand he takes away with the other. And on another trip to the city of New Orleans, as noted in *Prose Works:*

> One of my choice amusements during my stay in New Orleans was going down to the old French Market, especially of a Sunday morning. The show was a varied and curious one; among the rest, the Indian and negro hucksters with their wares. For there were always fine specimens of Indians, both men and women, young and old. I remember I nearly always on these

occasions got a large cup of delicious coffee with a biscuit, for my breakfast, from the immense shining copper kettle of a great Creole mulatto (I believe she weigh'd 230 pounds).

The utterance of a typical American tourist traveling in foreign lands, this paragraph sounds as if Whitman were attending the farmers' market browsing for fresh summer tomatoes or early ears of corn, not consorting with human beings—even though he's thoroughly fascinated with the color and gaiety of the French Quarter, as any tourist would be.

Whitman produced a few minor poems concerning Indians. He recorded the deaths of both Red Jacket and Osceola. In "Red Jacket" he writes:

> Upon this scene, this show,
> Yielded to-day by fashion, learning, wealth,
> (Nor in caprice alone—some grains of deepest
>   meaning,)
> Haply, aloft, (who knows?) from distant sky-
>   clouds' blended shapes,
> As some old tree, or rock or cliff, thrill'd with its
>   soul,
> Product of Nature's sun, stars, earth direct—a
>   towering human form,
> In hunting-shirt of film, arm'd with the rifle, a
>   halfironical smile curving its phantom lips,
> Like one of Ossian's ghosts looks down.

Ossian, of course, was a legendary Gaelic bard of the third century often denounced as the pure fakery of James Macpherson when he published the collection *Fingal*. Red Jacket was sixty-three years old when Whitman was born and so to him Red Jacket and his deeds during the American Revolution could hardly be considered "legendary." Red Jacket's skill as a warrior was minimal. He was teased by both Cornplanter and Joseph Brant for his cowardice in battle and failure to attend the battles. His importance to the Iroquois Confederacy and to the British, especially during the American Revolution, was as an orator and politician. How odd that in this verse Red Jacket stands "arm'd with the rifle" and not the quill. Surely Whitman would have known these salient facts concerning Red Jacket, who in his time was widely acclaimed as an Indian leader. It supports the fact that Whitman was an uncritical Rousseauian romanticist, not well up on current events, or an outright racist. His collected writings seem to suggest all three at varying times.

Osceola doesn't fare much better than Red Jacket in Whitman's verse "Osceola":

> Painted half his face and neck, his wrists, and
>   backhands,
> Put the scalp-knife carefully in his belt—then
>   lying down, resting a moment,
> Rose again, half sitting, smiled, gave in silence
>   his extended hand to each and all,
> Sank faintly low to the floor (tightly grasping
>   the tomahawk handle,)
> Fix'd his look on wife and little children—the
>   last:
> (And here a line in memory of his name and
>   death.)

In an epigraph, Whitman states that Osceola died of "a broken heart." Most historians agree he died of malaria or possibly from being poisoned or from maltreatment. Later his head was cut off and placed on display in the Medical Museum. At the time of his death, Osceola was thirty-four and Whitman was nearing twenty. A U.S. marine was the poet's informant, a boy he'd met one day in Brooklyn.

He wrote "Yonnondio," an Iroquois lament, and in the poem "The Sleepers" he devoted a passage to an Indian "squaw," though she was a somewhat supernatural being who appeared before his mother: "She remember'd her many a winter and many a summer, / But the red squaw never came nor was heard of there again." Whitman was obviously unaware that the word "squaw" was a derogatory term that referred to a woman's reproductive organs. It did not signify an Indian woman as such. And there are other scattered passages, but Whitman basically held the "doomed" Indian as not a fit subject for verse. Indians neither produced nor were produced by Whitman's hero, America, and merited only a veiled apparition or pitiful elegy.

Whitman, however, immortalized General George Armstrong Custer in the elegy "From Far Dakota's Canyons," within which Custer died "bearing a bright sword in thy hand, / Now ending well in death the splendid fever of thy deeds"—deeds such as killing Indians manipulated through surprise attacks for self-aggrandizement and for the federal government. As a poem it is not successful; as an elegy it borders on the maudlin; as history it is about as accurate as Keats attributing the discovery of the Pacific Ocean to Cortes.

In his collection of daily jottings, *Specimen Days*, Whitman noted in August 1881 his viewing of John Mulvany's painting of Custer's fall at the Little Big Horn. The poet lamented, pathetically, that he had but an hour to spend in thought before this "vast canvas" with "swarms upon swarms of savage Sioux, in their war-bonnets, frantic...driving through the background, through the smoke, like a hurricane of demons." Mulvany's painting, *Custer's Last Rally,* was "all native, all our own, and all a fact." It was American, not native in an indigenous sense. Only America could produce a spectacular event of such heroic proportions. Whitman, apparently, was a proponent of the manifest destiny bilge of the earlier decades and still of his current day. While there is no overt condemnation of Indians, there is also no understanding of what the "rally" was all about. His was a simple case of hero worship and adulation of the legendary boy-general and his glossy curls. Perhaps Whitman had read too many penny novels. "Custer (his hair cut short) stands in the middle, with dilated eye and extended arm, aiming a huge cavalry pistol." In "From Far Dakota's Canyons," the poet had Custer's hair "flowing" and portrayed the general "leaving behind [him] a memory sweet to soldiers." This does not sound like the "Hard-backsides" or "Iron-ass" many of those soldiers remembered. There is some doubt that his own men, such as Marcus Reno or Fred Benteen, would retain a "sweet" memory of the suicidal young general who had been labeled a murderer of his own soldiers by his staff.

Even in 1876, strangely, in America many important authors did not accept the fact that Custer brought about his own defeat and demise in the direct attack on the Lakota (Sioux) and Cheyenne peaceful encampment at Little Big Horn on that hot June morning. Most sensible historians today conclude that Custer was in total error when foolishly attacking this encampment which outnumbered his troops. This fact had been repeatedly spelled out to the general by various scouts in his command. As Mari Sandoz suggests in *The Battle of the Little Bighorn*, 1876 was an election year and killing Indians in the Far West could easily catapult his missile-star high in the skies before the eyes of the American public about to select, nominate the next candidate for president. His aim in this attack, not battle, was to revive the American sentiment. Custer's last major campaign was in 1868, eight years prior to the Little Big Horn. The public is fickle and prone to forgetfulness. He needed headlines and consequently brought along his own newspaper reporter. Knowing full well the odds against him, knowing also the American public's deep desire for heroism and heroes, he chose to attack an encampment of nearly 10,000 Indians with a handful of soldiers—many raw recruits, some drunk on whiskey, and many frightened and angry that their commander would knowingly lead them to their deaths. The daredevil never faltered. He marched his men into glory, into history, and into Whitman's imagination ready and willing to accept the boy-general as hero and champion of the people, his "average bulk."

All nations are in need of cultural heroes, hence, Ulysses and Aeneas, Virginia Dare of Roanoake and George Washington. Custer had his Homer, his Virgil. In Whitman, however, not only are the poem and the essay both inaccurate, they also are creatively weak in execution and language and do not survive as a major work of art befitting the honor of epic. Nor is Custer a proven cultural hero. He did not save the day, let alone the men under his command. What he accomplished, apart from his demise, was to start a controversy which continues to rage to this moment.

Whitman describes, again in *Specimen Days,* an extended trip to the Far West in autumn of 1879. The poet, while traveling the plains among the ghosts of legendary chiefs, never mentions the historical fact that those lands were once inhabited by Indians. The word "Indian" is not used. Strange.

I cannot but wonder where Whitman's thoughts lay at the Camp Grant Massacre or the Sand Creek Massacre or the flight of the Nez Perce. How is it that Geronimo, Roman Nose, Crazy Horse, and Chief Joseph were not fit subjects for epics, great warriors and heroes to their people which they indeed are? Whitman was not the only major poet of his day to slight these heroes. Whittier, Emerson, Lowell, and Lanier all ignored them.

But Whitman's life-style, thought, poetic vision, and sympathies were with the common American, so he could be expected to hold strong feelings for the plight of a mighty race of human beings crushed under the impervious foot of the imperialism of mechanical progress. Not until the twentieth century did poets fully realize the essential value and quality of that culture so readily put to the gun.

It is a tragic loss that the American Indian did not prove a fit subject for Whitman's powerful poetics. Perhaps Whitman, with all his poetic power, might well have composed a truly immortal epic. He lived during the momentous time of the Plains Nations and the deaths of the Woodland Nations. Obviously, for whatever personal reasons, Whitman closed his ears and shut his eyes to the Indians' death cries. Much to literature's and history's loss, he turned his back on this American tragedy.

Sitting Bull, Rain-in-the-face, Black Kettle, Roman Nose, and their brothers and sisters still await a courageous poet to recreate their lives and deeds, their monumental strengths and successes, and their suffering in verse, for the eyes and ears of the world. Perhaps their own living sons and daughters will take up the pen. Whitman's indifference failed them.

Not to Forget

Drawing-room novelist James Fenimore Cooper could not have spotted an Indian in the forest if retaining his scalp depended on it. The still vividly readable historian Francis Parkman's aversion to Indians was as pronounced as that of Benjamin Franklin and George Washington. Whittier was drawn to "the naked savage" more to honor the demise of the boy-general commonly known to his officers and recruits as "hard-ass Custer" than for any heart-felt understanding of the Plains peoples' tragic plight. His infamous poem, "Rain-in-the-Face," helped propagate the concept of the "blood-thirsty redskin" hell-bent on mayhem and murder. He ignored Sitting Bull and the other great men and women of the Plains who fought so admirably for life and land and against a programmed genocide. Like his colleagues, Whittier was blinded by, among other things, the ideology of the manifest destiny bilge. One would expect Walt Whitman to have had a more compassionate soul. But Whitman, who worked in the office of the Bureau of Indian Affairs, was also caught up in the propaganda of the time: when Indians were conquerable, they were not romantic subjects for poetry. Custer—handsome, Byronic, but decidely neurotic—remained Whitman's hero to the end. This leaves the great, bearded Longfellow, who meant well, one could suppose, but so confused issues, ideas, locales, and characters in Hiawatha that it is pointless to read his work for insight on Native American life. These authors—excluding Parkman, who did venture into the far West in search of the "real McCoy"—had little or no direct contact with either an Indian village or the culture. They were arm-chair thieves.

These authors were not only high romantics but they believed in a double standard of democracy, not unlike the philosophy of their forefather, Thomas Jefferson, who believed that democracy was for the white, landed gentry. He wanted to solve the "Indian problem" through genocide, leaving the few who remained to stagnate in the death camps otherwise known as reservations. Few of these writers heard the death-knell nor the cries of the dying. It is difficult, indeed, to understand how these sensitive authors could turn their heads to this death and continue to write their novels and poems as the fires of the villages were extinguished one by one. They have all been excused by the literary guardians and historians as having been powerless to defend the right to life, liberty, and the pursuit of happiness—ideas most prominent in those times.

It was not until 1881, when Helen Hunt Jackson published *A Century of Dishonor,* that a major work appeared to challenge the status quo. It remains in print to this day, due mainly to the fact that the status quo has not been challenged sufficiently. *A Century of Dishonor* is by no means creative literature. It remains stylized history written in dense language and marred by difficult flowery images. But it was strongly flavored by humanitarianism and did inflame minds and manage to make visible wrongs done to a desparate people. Jackson was one in a handful of acutely sensitive intellectuals of her time.

Of those other authors of the early decades of this century, and into the middle-years, such as Vachel Lindsay (who thumped his chest and chanted rhetoric to unsophisticated audiences believing he sang the real, the true, the authentic), Mary Austin (who sweetly translated from anthropologists' thievings), and Hart Crane (who yodeled from the top spire of the Brooklyn Bridge), perhaps only the novels of William Faulkner bear any resemblance to what an Indian is really like. Hemingway, that great outdoorsman, ignored not only America but its original caretakers.

In 1932 John G. Neihardt published *Black Elk Speaks*, subtitled, B*eing the Life Story of a Holy Man of the Oglala Sioux.* Black Elk spoke a hesitant English and Neihardt spoke little, if any, Lakota, so a translator bridged their minds. The translation was transcribed by Neihardt's daughter and edited by Neihardt himself. What we have is an incredibly beautiful book, a book which Vine Deloria, Jr. has suggested may well be the only important religious book to have been published thus far in America. It is, however, a book authored by Neihardt, not Black Elk, and it can only be speculated how much poetic license Neihardt took with Black Elk's words. This book has probably been the most influential book to be published in America on Indian subjects. During the 1960s and '70s there was hardly a university student who did not study it in the classroom, and it became an important counter-culture tract during the Vietnam war.

Frank Waters, an Anglo who lived in the Southwest during the 1930s, worked in both anthropology and fiction. His books on the Hopi and Navajo proved successful at bookstores, and his novel, *The Man Who Killed the Deer,* remains a classic, as does LaFarge's *Laughing Boy.* Both books offered sensible insights on Indian life.

Also in the 1930s and '40s, when not many editors had an interest in Indian materials, Mari Sandoz, an author respected by

Native American writers, wrote as honestly of history as she knew how—and wrote not merely well but brilliantly. She discovered the difficulty of publishing early in her career. She said in her autobiographical sketches that it took seventy-five essays before she was first accepted for publication. Probably best known for her biography of her father, *Old Jules,* her picture of life on the prairie at the turn of the century caused something of a stir. Her most influencial books are *Cheyenne Autumn* (1953) and the biography of the Lakota warrior, *Crazy Horse (1942).*

Another great splash was made in 1961 when Theodora Krober, widow of anthropologist and linguist Alfred Krober, published the tragic story of Ishi, which was promoted by its publisher as "the story of the last wild Indian in North America." Ishi is the story of a people and their extinction by ranchers and gold miners alike in the foothills of the Sierras. Driven first into those hills, they were then hounded down and coldly murdered in dark caves, where mothers futilely covered the bodies of their children with their own. A few managed to escape deeper into the forest and stubbornly fought to survive, and to survive with culture intact. On a morning in 1911, a rancher's dog found a human being dying from starvation. It was Ishi, the last of his tribe. He was soon brought to metropolitan San Francisco to be studied, where he was incarcerated in the Berkeley Museum of Anthropopogy and displayed for tourists. He remained in this glass cage until his death on March 25, 1916. Although somewhat romantically written, the book did ignite the country.

At about the same time, another American writer was finishing a novel—perhaps the best novel to date written by a non-Indian on Indian themes, Thomas Berger's *Little Big Man.* Unlike Longfellow, Berger did his homework. His research is impressively accurate. Berger first thought of his novel as being a satire on the far west, but it developed into a tragic story of human frailty. Berger presented the Indians as human beings, with both good and bad attributes. The book remained on the bestseller list in 1964 for months, and its success paved the way for the even larger success of Dee Brown's history, *Bury My Heart at Wounded Knee,* and socialist Peter Farb's *Man's Rise to Civilization.*

Brown's history was not only romanticized but was occasionally inaccurate and based, again, primarily upon non-Indian records. Brown, for a time, became the self-appointed spokesman for the Native American to America. Most Indians laughed at him or simply shrugged their shoulders and turned to a good smoke. Brown's and Farb's books remained on the bestseller lists for many months, however, and it was only then that major publishers began to glimpse the gold to be mined in Native American literature.

Contemporary American Literature it seemed, held that last vestige of Manifest Destiny: the right to conquer, the right to the spoils of war. But it wasn't land being usurped this time; it was culture and spirit. The Hopi/Miwok poet, Wendy Rose, writing in 1981 in a small press magazine symposium on Native American Literature, *Poetry Flash,* stated:

> It is with a sense of irony that I see the literary world greet Native American writers in such a way as to make it seem as if a "new" literature were coming into view. Even the most "established" Indian writers are never quite "established" enough, but are condemned to the status of literary exotica for the duration of their careers with their publications relegated to the

"anthropology" or "juvenile" shelves in libraries and bookstores regardless of content or style. Literary analysts and critics have said that there has been a "renaissance" of Indian writing, especially poetry, between 1969 and 1976—and it is true there was a flurry of interest expressed in the publication of token anthologies by all the major presses. The flurry was also expressed in the increasing numbers of "white shamans" that donned masks, beads and feathers to use what they imagined (wrongly) to be native poetic forms and motifs. It is a further irony that some poets gained their greatest fame in this cultural and professional rip-off. All the time that this was going on, there were genuine Indian writers whose work was largely ignored except for the above mentioned anthologies most of which have disappeared without so much as a whimper. Like the majority of poets, Indian poets' publications tended to appear in small presses with little funding and were doomed to obscurity through severely limited distribution. And, like other poets, their work represented the total spectrum in style and quality. It is at this point, perhaps, that I should emphatically state that there is no such genre as "Indian Poetry." There is only poetry written by Indian people.

There has always been a singular attraction in this country to the "primitive," whether jazz, gospel or Indian/Shamanism.

Museums spend incredible amounts of money acquiring pre-Columbian art. Anthropologists and archaeologists gain international reputation; novelists are fawned over by Hollywood producers. Vine Deloria, Jr. has written that every thirty years or so an interest in "Indian," and particularly Indian literature, flames. There is a stampede to the mountains for gold, often driven by absolute greed, although sometimes there is a genuine *simpatico* and an historical, anthropological, or even critical interest in explaining what may not, in fact, be explainable. In the 1960s and '70s, as Miss Rose suggested, these mountains were bulldozed. The gold was often extracted in perverted ruthlessness without any consideration for property, let alone for sacred rite, privacy, or human feeling. The 1973 confrontation at Pine Ridge/Wounded Knee captured headlines in *The New York Times* and was given prime time on every major network evening news program, as was the seige at Alcatraz Island in 1969. The public and the media waited with bated breath for the Native Americans to shed blood, yet the bloodshed was caused mainly by various government agencies. Both Alcatraz and Wounded Knee scorched America into reconsidering the province of the Native Americans. Along with the broken treaties and the poverty on and off the reservations, white America suddenly saw the culture, the ceremonies, and the literature: prayer, song, and story. It awakened the country again to the concept of the great American frontier and to a people not yet completely tamed. The determination of those at Alcatraz Island and Wounded Knee to maintain their culture and their sovereignty in the face of such overwhelming odds spurred interest.

The rush was on. Reservations crawled with anthropologists, literary critics, novelists, poets, editors, cultists, hippies and the media. No tongue was left quiet, no house allowed to be closed, off-limits. There were no limits. Even Madison Avenue joined in: "You call it corn. We call it maize," a woman in Native costume smiled in one popular margarine commercial. During those years everyone, it seemed, wanted to be an Indian, though few aspired to be Asian or Black or any other minority. Revolution had taken the country by storm. The young were disenchanted, as were some of the older liberals. Institutions, they believed, had to be changed, if not completely torn down. Government needed to be overhauled like an automobile that failed to run smoothly on new super highways. There were bloody protests, and escapes. The young went to the woods, some to Canada in the face of the illegal war in Vietnam. And some went to "Indianism," determined to become, to use an ugly phrase, "Squawmen." Many non-Indian Americans found Native American great-grandmothers in the closet.

On the reservations and in city ghettos, a spirit, free and rich in culture was found. A few editors, though they were suspect as well, sought poets and storytellers, mainly young at first. These editors traveled to the Institute of American Indian Art in Santa Fe, New Mexico, and from there to the reserves, where they discovered gold: Simon J. Ortiz at Acoma, Leslie Marmon Silko at Laguna, Lance Henson in Oklahoma, Peter Blue Cloud in the California Sierras, Wendy Rose in Oakland, N. Scott Momaday at Stanford University. Hundreds of small press publishers brought out thin chapbooks in limited editions of such young poets as Rose, Henson, Peter Blue Cloud, Paula Gunn Allen, Duane Niatum, Gladys Cardiff, Karoniaktatie, and many others

"Indianism" was gold. No self-respecting editor, including those at the *American Poetry Review*, the *New Yorker,* the *Atlantic Monthly*, or *Poetry Magazine* could possibly go to press without a poem by at least one Indian. It was drums and feathers.

1969, the year of the Alcatraz seige, was also an important date in Native American letters. N. Scott Momaday, a Kiowa Indian, was awarded the Pulitzer Prize for his novel, *House Made of Dawn*, and Hyemeyohsts Storm published *Seven Arrows*. The incredible popularity and success of *Seven Arrows* upon its appearance was a major factor in the boom in Indian literature. The vast sums of money it earned for its publisher, Harper & Row, caused other major publishing houses to jump on the bandwagon with anthologies of Native American writing. Viking published *The Man to Send Rainclouds* (fiction, 1974), and *Voices of the Rainbow* (poetry, 1975). Random House printed *From the Belly of the Shark* (1973), which contained a heavy emphasis on traditional Native prayers and contemporary poetry. Of these anthologies, only one was edited by an Indian: Niatum had been hired by Harper and Row to edit his brilliant anthology *Carriers of the Dream Wheel* (1975).

Reputations were made with these various publications, leading Doubleday to print Janet Campbell-Hale's *Owl Song*, Harper & Row to bring out James Welch's *Winter in the Blood (1974)* and Ortiz's collection of poetry, *Going for the Rain (1976)*, and Viking to publish Silko's *Ceremony (1977)*.

Within these years others worked incessantly at these mines, not without a modicum of altruistic intent, yet not void of foresight into literary history. In northern New York State, in the village of Hogansburg at the St. Regis Reserve, Akwesasne, Rarihokwats (Jerry Gamble) was publishing the Mohawk newspaper, *Akwesasne Notes* with aid from the Mohawk people of the locale: journalists, artists, poets, office workers, cooks and woodchoppers. Gary Snyder was publishing the poems which would be collected into his Pulitzer Prize-winning, *Turtle Island*, published late in 1974. Jerome Rothenberg was working and writing in Salamanca, a village on the Seneca Cattarugus Reserve in western New York state, and in 1978 published his collection of poems, *A Seneca Journal*. Rothenberg, with co-editor Dennis Tedlock, also published two major anthologies, *Technicians of the Sacred* and *Shaking the Pumpkin*, and an ethno-poetic journal, *Alcheringa*.

For ten years mountains were mined, and then, as suddenly as it had commenced, interest in Native American writing ceased, as though the gold had given out. The miners retreated back to the editors' desks and the universities. Harper & Row was no longer interested in looking at manuscripts for its now inactive Native American Publishing Program. The *New York Times* went back to sleep. The gold had been mined. Small fortunes were made by various participants. Yet, the only Native American author I'm aware of who received a share of the gold was Momaday. As usual, it was the non-Indian writer, historian and publisher who took the spoils of war.

2/25/82

THE QUEST:
A MEDITATION ON NATURE AND MONUMENTS

For Native American people, there is a sacredness to mountains. The mountain peak is the place where young Native people go for the vision that will direct their life's path. Often the youth brings a gift, usually leaves of tobacco, sage, or cedar. Why a mountain rather than a lake, a desert valley, or the shore of a swift river? The mountain peak is the space on the earth closest to the spirit world above, where the ancestors and Creator dwell. Here you and the spirit beings meet through vision, dream, or, some might say, imagination. This quest is similar to Moses going to the mountain for the Ten Commandments or to Dr. Martin Luther King's dream quest on his metaphorical mountain. From whatever plain it may rise, in Asia Minor as in the Americas, the mountain holds special powers for many peoples, particularly tribal people.

This past fall, I drove west to a teaching residency in British Columbia with two young students who both hold a deep respect for the mountain. Our plan was to drive to South Dakota, through a corner of Wyoming, and north to Montana, where we would spend time at Glacier National Park. The highways to Glacier were dotted with fast food outlets, tire cemeteries, mini-market gas stations, used car lots and the like—what Henry

Miller described in the 1930s as the "air-conditioned nightmare." He could now add to the horrors on the land most of New Jersey; Gary, Indiana; the outskirts of Chicago; and just about any American city. In my many crossings since my first trip to California in 1963, America has become less vast, less spacious, less beautiful, and less sacred. It has become ugly. Nebraska looks like Pennsylvania, Iowa like Kansas. America has no respect for the calm, silent beauty of natural earth. This beauty is covered over. Beauty to America is the eyesore of Las Vegas, the abominable gaming casinos surrounded by a desert full of old tires, aluminum cans, and candy wrappers. The poetry has been obliterated from the cacti, the datura, the living creatures who wriggle across the dry earth at twilight. The blossoms of the desert are being trampled beneath the marching feet of progress.

In South Dakota, in the sacred Black Hills of the Sioux (Lakota) people, is a work of (according to the government and various tourist bureaus) art. Carved into the side of Mount Rushmore are the heads of four American presidents: Lincoln, Washington, Theodore Roosevelt and the philosophical slaveholder, Thomas Jefferson. How many millions of dollars went into excavating this mountainside? Are the sculptures art or propaganda? To me, Mount Rushmore is a tragic example of federal government thumbing its nose at the Native Americans of South Dakota. Their sacred hills were first stolen, then scarred with the sculpted heads of four presidents who did their utmost to destroy the culture, the very spirit and body of these indigenous peoples. It is an insult to the mountain and the sacredness of the Black Hills.

Custer's discovery of gold in the Black Hills opened the floodgates not only to prospectors but to all future generations of exploiters. This includes the government, which has shown so little respect for what is sacred to the Lakota people. A once-serene mountain range has been changed into a carnival, a Coney Island of the West. One would suppose that America needs its heros and myths, but need it destroy natural beauty to honor with artifice? Mount Rushmore has joined the jungle of golden arches, gas station standards, and billboards, cutting off the sight of that most pristine art, the natural world: green valleys, blue rivers, vast meadows, the majesty of mountains, even the sunrise and sunset.

Not far from Mount Rushmore, another mountain is under construction: the sculpting of an enormous stone into the likeness of the Lakota peace man, Crazy Horse. Coming down from the four stone presidents, we drove the few miles to see the Crazy Horse monument. In the moonlight, it was austere and inspiring. The winds were silent as though at prayer. Not a fox yip or wolf howl, not a single mechanical motor sputter nor foot crunching the cinders of the path. The night was a poem; the stone was a poem, the narrative epic of this great figure who fought for his people's freedom. Crazy Horse asked for nothing but a free life. He had no intention of building a vast empire of fast food chains, digging for oil or gold, declaring war, or building monuments on the mountainside. Warrior that he was, he dreamed always of the beauty of peace, the youthful vision quest, perhaps the buffalo hunt. The only art that filtered through his imagination was probably his spirit paint, perhaps the war paint on his own body as well as on that of his horse, paint which would wash away in the rain. Or he might have raised a scaffold for his dead, and even the scaffold would be decked with beauty, the art of burial: a simple structure on a flat cottonwood bough, a bier festooned with feathers, which would eventually return to the earth as dust, a cyclical art.

We left this developing monument exalted. We had seen the Corn Palace in South Dakota, the Badlands decorated with Kodak boxes, cigarette butts and Coke cans; we had seen hundreds of dead pheasants along the roads, the dude ranches on mountain slopes. But we left the Black Hills exalted. We had breathed the prayers of the winds and the moon shining on the tremendous stone that one day would be the shape of Crazy Horse riding his pony across a free and open prairie, at peace with the earth.

It is human nature to erect monuments, symbols of the age and of the great figures who created the age. But in our times, these monuments are billboards, flags on the moon, burnt forests, stripped or bulldozed mountains: desecration. It would be more fitting to leave a pinch of tobacco, a mound of dried corn, a prayer feather, a sand painting, to honor with something which will eventually be carried off by winds into the night, leaving the memory, a poem. The art of the mountain top ceremony—the vision quest—exemplifies the best interaction of art and environment. It blows away, until the next youth reaches the summit with his gift for the good spirits.

WAITING AT THE EDGE

Sometimes...Injustice

The day I was born my father bought me a .22.
A year later my mother
traded it for a violin.
Ten years later my big sister traded that
for a guitar, and gave it to her boyfriend...
who sold it.

Now you know why I never learned to hunt,
or learned how to play a musical instrument,
or became a Wall St. broker.

The Mama Poems
(White Pine Press, 1984)

I could easily have commenced this essay with any number of poems; however, I decided the one above was more apt than others dealing directly with either home in northern New York state and the Adirondacks or directly with Iroquois (Mohawk) ancestry or culture, which I have written about over many years. "Sometimes...Injustice" says for me, at least, where I was, where I was going, and pretty much how I was to get there. There is also a touch of humor—which is in short supply in my work—and it is a poem my father would enjoy were he alive to read it, though to this hour my big sister denies the guitar swap. It is a poem that leads me back in time to birth, childhood, and young manhood when I sporadically published feeble efforts in local newspapers. Yes, my mother traded the gun for a violin which I never learned to play, and my sister traded the violin for a guitar and gave it to the boyfriend—who later became her husband. And I never became a Wall Street broker but a hunter of words, of songs. I am still hunting.

Yet at this very moment the poem strikes me as an odd choice because I am sitting at a window staring out at the high peaks of the Adirondacks while "writer in residence" in Saranac Lake during the deer-hunting season. Bear season has just nicely closed, and deer opened this very morning. I am obliged to remember the mornings I would steal out and board my father's Chevy, snuggle behind the back seat, and hope my dad would not discover me until he reached the hunting woods. He was a fine hunter and rarely returned to my mother's kitchen without having bagged at least a "supper" rabbit, if not a deer, grouse, or pheasant. I don't remember him coming home with either a bear or moose. At that time moose still roamed the northern woods.

My father would have been proudly overjoyed had I, too, become a skilled hunter, though confidentially, I think he'd be satisfied to know that I have been a hunter of words and my game has been abundant. I have hunted not only words and images, metaphors, but, to my mother's relish, also song. I have heard the cedar sing, I have listened to the white pine, I have imitated white-tail deer and hawk and cocked an ear even to the more plain song of robin, a running brook, chicory weaving on summer winds. I have sung the round dance of the Longhouse—feet stomping the wooden floor, drum beating, singers' throats throbbing. I have sung the *adowe,* I have wailed at death, I have chortled at weddings, I have attempted to lyric all the sounds of the earth, not only of us two-legged but of the four-legged, the winged, and those of the waters.

I have laid open my complete self to all those sounds, those musical notes of birth and death and all that happens between, whether it be the sighting of woodchucks sunning on the edges of the Mohawk River, the bend of a mullein, the trot of wolf across cold winter hills, the four winds and directions themselves, the fruit hanging on my sister's sour cherry tree, my niece Martha's apple orchard, my ever-so-great-grandfather Joshua Clark's entry into the bowels of northern New York where he founded the first Baptist Church and where his loins eventually produced my mother, who also came from good Seneca (Parker) stock. I have sung the Adirondacks—the death of its rivers and blue lakes from acid rain. How odd when something kills what it first helped create—like in Greek tragedy. I have sung the mountains with their rising peaks, packs of coy-dogs, bear, the mountains' history and future. Yes, I have been a hunter of song. My father taught me well, how to hold my .22, to aim, when to pull the trigger, and, last, how to skin out my game.

This mid-October, I sit here at the window staring out at birch, white pine, sugar maple, all rather drenched this morning from last night's rain—unsullied, one hopes, by the midwestern industrial acids that are killing the mountains and all the life upon these mountains. A grey squirrel rushes up and down an oak tree; his mouth is crammed with a large acorn. He stops, flicks his tail at the sound of this typewriter's racket, and scuttles up the trunk. I sit at this window, the lake a brief walk down the hill.

I sit in this window within a house called "Tamarack House." Not a tree house, it houses students of the community college where I am resident. Some of the students from Tamarack House are in the wet woods now tracking the white-tail deer, hoping for a venison feast, a venison which probably none of them have the faintest inkling of how to prepare and cook. They are mainly from big cities, and, being freshmen and new to these magical mountain woods, they've\ never hunted before—not bear, not white-tails, and especially not word-songs.

I was a shy child, the youngest of three and an only male. My sisters were not only pretty but rather smart and certainly talented. They both sang with quite lovely voices and played the piano with some small gift, having been taught by an elderly neighbor whom we called "Aunt Flo," though she was no relation. A former schoolmarm and spinster who loved children, she thoroughly enjoyed seeing that some art—book reading and piano playing—entered their lives. Aunt Flo was instrumental in opening many doors for me and especially for my older sister— the sister who traded my violin for a guitar—who to this day sings professionally in a chorus in St. Louis. Aunt Flo gave me respect for the written word; my father gave me respect for the hunt, the game itself, the woods.

My mother did not actually place such instruments in my young palms; she did, however, give me a prophecy, a tea reading. When I was a mere slip, my mother went to a fortuneteller and had her tea leaves read. I stood near the gypsy, or what I took to be a gypsy; she stared blankly at me. I was probably sucking my thumb and wailing to go home. She ignored my mother's future and exposed mine. I remember her saying, "I see him, that little fellow there, I see him holding books or rocks. But I think it is books. He holds many of them. Things are spilling out of them. Pictures. Will he be a painter? He will be verrrrry famouuuuuuse." Well, I didn't become a painter but a painter of word pictures, though as a teenager I did dabble, unsuccessfully, with oils. I had no sense of draftsmanship. I couldn't draw the straight side of a barn, let alone the flight of an eagle or the head of a horse. My paintings were quite reminiscent of Grandma Moses. I had seen many reproductions of her paintings and enjoyed them. I duplicated, and it wasn't difficult, but it was certain I had no talent, even though my father encouraged this painting, neighbors bought a canvas or two, and I was offered the opportunity to take drawing classes. The prediction had been made. I was to hold books or rocks. Naturally, the preference became books.

It is only fair that I mention here that my sister was a good storyteller of ghost tales on a summer eve when bats flew low and fireflies lit the darkness. I recognized fairly soon that I should never become a teller of tales. I possessed neither the knack nor the memory to record, let alone invent, them. Traditionally, stories are told in the depths of winter when the village is safe from ambush and the work of both men and women is completed for the long cold. Game is stored with dried corn and fruit. Then there is time to relax, to sit back and listen to stories, to be entertained and to be instructed, as traditional stories are teaching instruments for sharing knowledge and practical know-how. My sister's stories were merely told to scare the beans out of us. No teaching was ever intended. I have asked her many times to tell those stories she told when we were children, but she claims she long ago forgot them.

As I said, I was a shy boy. My sisters' talents did not help me to get over my inadequacies. I knew I was a hunter. I knew also that the songs my father sang on Friday night, particularly when encouraged by a few bottles of beer or a pint of Christian Brothers brandy, were greatly to my liking. One song from Friday nights I remember, as he sang it continually, went thus: "If I had the wings of a turtle, over these prison walls I would fly." Turtles don't have wings. And turtles weren't, as far as my young mind knew, incarcerated. Was he speaking of turtle doves? No, he meant turtles. Mud turtles. Turtles in the pond at my Aunt Jennie's farm. Turtles in the minute lake where I used to go play on "Witches' Hill" in the foothills of the Adirondacks where I grew up.

These many years later I think my father felt he was jailed, imprisoned, even though, to the best of my knowledge, he was literally jailed briefly only once on a drunk charge and for recklessly driving the old Chevy. There were things he desired to do, accomplish, and places he fervently desired to go, to see—such as Alaska and the blossomed cherry trees in Washington, D.C.— though he constantly instructed that there was no place more beautiful than northern New York state. That was a lesson which took some years for me to learn, digest, and agree with. He died before he saw the cherry trees, or Alaska. Though he had had the opportunity of only the first two grades of school, my father was a clever, sharp, and, in a homespun fashion, intelligent man— though he did have a hard time understanding his children, as did my mother. He rose from being the water boy on a ditchdigging crew to being foreman, and eventually gave up a comfortable job working for the city to open and operate his own business, a restaurant and a small chain of three gas stations. When he died in 1958, he was comfortably solvent. But all those years he felt imprisoned. I'd suppose that only when he tracked the woods or boated the lake fishing did he feel free, unfettered, alive.

> My father wades the morning river
> tangled in the colors of the dawn.

from "My Sixth August"

Surely, because my father found so much beauty and joy in the woods and the lakes and rivers, I too found this same beauty and freedom. And because Aunt Flo was never able to coordinate my fingers to the keys of her piano, and because my older sisters teased my singing voice (I was, naturally, a boy soprano), I, too, took to walking lone and free near those same rivers and creeks, through those meadows and fields, and within those dark but green woods that my father trailed. It was there I could sing, sing to wrens and larks, maples and cedars, fox and rabbits. I learned, walking these meadows edging the woods, crossed by the various streams, that I could make up songs not merely of my loneness but of the loneness and the beauty of these other creatures, and could actually write these songs down on paper. My first poems were composed.

I was born on the hottest night of August in 1929—so hot my mother always claimed she could not remember the hour, though I have a strong feeling that it was late—in a small town nesting in the foothills of the Adirondacks on the shores of Black River, which flows out of the mountains and into the great Lake Ontario. The day I was born my father bought me that .22 and gave me a hound dog. Happy was his name. I was born a blue baby two months early, already confronting the vicissitudes of life; eczema blemished my skin. I suffered this horrific rash most of my childhood and painfully remember too well going to bed with my hands tied in mittens to prevent my scratching open the skin. And I was not only found to be allergic to eggs, which to this moment disturbs some of the joys of living, but I also had a weak chest and was prone to hay fever. I loved the haying in the summer fields and playing in the high haylofts. Adults who came and went in our house sneered at these allergies: I was making them up as little boys are often wont, seeking attention. They played games by tempting me to down an egg and offered me a nickel if I could keep a hard-boiled egg in my stomach. (It proved impossible.) They would give me a pudding or a slice of cake pretending it was eggless, yet I retched the moment the sweet reached the stomach. Of course, these allergies helped make me feel different, an outcast. Neither my sisters nor my friends seemed to have these physical problems. It helped make me the loner.

I spent my summers at one of three places: either my Aunt Jennie's farm (my mother's old homestead) on Fox Creek Road in the township of Cape Vincent; my father's lakeside cabin on Chaumont Bay; or my Uncle Eugene's farm in Canada near Verona and Enterprise, a strongly Catholic community of heavy Irish drinkers. I intensely disliked my uncle's house. He was a prankster and thoroughly enjoyed seeing me stew, lose my temper, and cry for my father to come retrieve me from his—as I thought—fiendish clutches. He once made my life there so miserable that I physically struck him. He whipped me in the field with my two cousins, his sons, watching. My father arrived shortly, whipped me a second time for disrespecting my uncle, his half brother, and took me back to the States, where I was shipped to my aunt's farm in Cape Vincent. I remember it vividly. It was my birthday when I arrived, and her neighbor baked me a surprise cake with pink frosting. I took a bite and became instantly ill. That was probably my worst summer. I sang out my heart and made good friends with my aunt's old mongrel dog, his lack of pedigree being most apt for the occasion. I felt bedraggled, outlawed, imprisoned.

It is quite unusual for Indian parents to whip children. It is thought the child learns better by example, hence the teaching stories. My father rarely whipped his children, but when he did it was almost with a vengeance and that usually on beer-night Fridays.

All this summer traveling, shifting-about, farming us out to various family members, helped develop my wanderlust, my own discord with settling, my varied and sometimes erratic travel, my impatient need to be on the go, to settle back in the seat of either a Greyhound bus or an Amtrak rail car. My father never suspected that my desire to roam was partially due to his shifting us about. He could not come to grips with my wanderings.

Obviously, my father and his lifestyle influenced my life. It's odd because early in my youth I figured it was my mother who so strongly affected me. It was perhaps only twenty years ago that I came to this astounding realization. I thought I was running away from my father's influence, and the opposite was true. I was running toward it, deeply into it. Though from time to time I have lived in large metropolitan cities or in foreign countries, I was seeking the blossoming cherry trees and Alaska that he never got to see, even though as yet I have not seen those trees nor visited Alaska. I have always been running home—my father's thought—which I fully recognize now as being that warm fireside or bosom of "home." Place is an extremely important theme in my poetry, and I have been questioned many times where that place, that home is. Is it northern New York with mountains and rivers, woods and fields; is it the reservation, the town in which I grew up; or is it Brooklyn, where I currently live? (I'm only passing through Saranac Lake.) Is it Albuquerque, which I deeply enjoy visiting; Berkeley, where my life's best friend lives? Is it Mexico, which I love most next to northern New York? Or is it on the Greyhound bus passing through this land that has been called "America," which I prefer calling, if it must be named, "The earth on turtle's back"? My father never spoke of this beautiful land as being America but as being home, and said that there was no place like it and that one day I would come to that truth, that realization, that positive fact. I would accept home and place, and be content. Save the cherry trees for dreaming, for wishes to be fulfilled.

So where is this place that I write of? Is it the foothills of the Adirondacks, the Lake Ontario summer cabin, my aunt's farm on Fox Creek Road, the reservation on the St. Lawrence River? Is it the woods or the fields growing wild strawberries so sweet to the tongue? Is it where I was born, where my first cry rent the night of that hot August? Is it the Brooklyn apartment I share with my cat, Sula? Is it with Kaherawaks, my surrogate granddaughter, at Akwesasne? Or is it a stuffy bus traveling the night highways across turtle's back? It is all of these places and things. It is even, yes, even the poems themselves, the persons I have created of wolf or berry, my ancestors such as Molly Brant or Ely Parker; my Aunt Jennie, old and now slightly feeble, but still driving the northern roads selling Avon products because when she stops she knows her life ends; my mother, whose own life-pain is with me still; my father's dreams and victories; my sisters and their lives; and my first tricycle that a cousin wrecked for me on the railroad track, my first red fire engine; the first pencil Aunt Flo placed in my hand when the piano intimidated those fingers of that hand. The "place" is within me and all around—whoever I touch, wherever I travel. It is not the personal "I" but the collective, because I wish all peoples to relate to that "I," become that "I" and find their place now that I have mine.

Wild Strawberry
for Helene

And I rode the Greyhound down to Brooklyn
where I sit now eating woody strawberries
grown on the backs of Mexican farmers
imported from the fields of their hands,
juices without color or sweetness.

my wild blood berries of spring meadows
sucked by June bees and protected by hawks
have stained my face and honeyed
my tongue...healed the sorrow in my flesh

vines crawl across the grassy floor
of the north, scatter to the world
seeking the light of the sun and innocent
tap of the rain to feed the roots
and bud small white flowers that in June
will burst fruit and announce spring
when wolf will drop winter fur
and wrens will break the egg

my blood, blood berries that brought laughter
and the ache in the stooped back that vied
with dandelions for the plucking,

and the wines nourished our youth
and heralded
iris, corn and summer melon
we fought bluebirds for the seeds
armed against garter snakes, field mice;
won the battle with the burning sun
which blinded our eyes and froze our hands
to the vines and the earth where knees knelt
and we laughed in the morning dew like worms
and grubs; we scented age and wisdom

my mother wrapped the wounds of the world
with a sassafras poultice and we ate
wild berries with their juices running
down the roots of our mouths and our joy

I sit here in Brooklyn eating Mexican
berries which I did not pick, nor do
I know the hands which did, nor their stories...
January snow falls, listen...

from *Dancing Back Strong the Nation*
(White Pine Press, 1981)

I began this poem in the winter of 1978. January to be exact, living in Brooklyn Heights in New York City; I was ill. A close friend and nearby neighbor had the goodness of heart and thought to bring to my sick bed a basket of cultivated strawberries. Helene knew my fondness for the fruit and just how important the strawberry is to me and my poetry. The wild strawberry

135

is not only the first natural fruit of the eastern spring, but it is the symbol of life to Iroquois people. The strawberry holds strong significance for all the people of the Six Nations and for me as a person, as a Mohawk writer, and as both editor and publisher. In 1976 I established Strawberry Press to be an exclusively Native American press to publish the poetry and art of Native People. There were, and remain still today, other Native Americans who publish Indian writing, but not exclusively. Joseph Bruchac of the *Greenfield Review* and Press, of Abnaki descent himself, indeed publishes many Native American writers, and it may well be the press's thrust; but he also publishes Black, Chicano, Asian, Anglo, and African writers. William Oandasan, Yuki/Filipino, of *"A" Magazine* and Press, likewise prints the works of a multicultural group of authors. Brother Benet Tvedten, deserving high praise for his *Blue Cloud Quarterly* and Press, has published more Native American writers, and others on related subjects, than anyone. Yet Brother Benet is of Swedish abstraction.

As I rallied from the illness, and while biting into those cultivated berries, sucking juices, I began to realize, to remember the many mornings of my childhood at home in northern New York state when I would follow my mother and two older sisters into the flowering fields where the wild strawberry vines crawled under the sun.

Strawberrying

morning
broods
   in the wide river
Mama bends

light
bleeds
always
in her day of
picking
(our fields are stained)
the moon, bats
tell us
to go
in the scent of
berries
fox
awaken
in stars

from *Kneading the Blood,*
(Strawberry Press, 1981)

With their children, other women, often my mother's friends, would be there picking and filling their baskets. It was a good time. Burning hot as it was in those open meadows, breezes did rush the grasses and flowers from off either Lake Ontario or the St. Lawrence River. It was a time of laughter, jokes and teasing, cries and tears from children bored with the labor and eager for a river swim. It was certainly not only a time of filling the belly with the deliciously honeysweet fruit, dripping in ripeness, but a time when the women exchanged what I thought were stories, gossip. I am convinced that was the reason they came to the fields. Even then, in 1934-35, those many years back, cultivated berries could be bought at roadside stands or in the village markets.

Also while eating the berries in my sick bed I recalled a strong sentiment of the Lakota Holy Man, Black Elk:

> When the ceremony was over, everybody felt a great deal better, for it had been a day of fun. They were better able now to see the greenness of the world, the wideness of the sacred day, the colors of the earth, and to set these in their minds.

Black Elk Speaks
(University of Nebraska Press, 1979)

There is no doubt in my mind that picking wild strawberries was a ceremony, and to this day it has offered me a better look at the grasses of the world, the width of a sacred day, and certainly the "colors of the earth." Picking those berries enriched not only our everyday lives and bellies but our imaginations and spirits as well. We all, even the children, truly felt better later. I wanted to write of this good feeling, this betterment and enrichment.

This year, winter 1983, strawberries were shipped air freight to the United States from Chile, in South America—a long way from the home meadows of the north. Obviously, air-freighted fruit must be harvested rather green and needs to complete the cycle en route. And, so, too, the berries in the basket that Helene had brought to me in January of 1978. The straw basket was stamped with purple ink: "Hecho En Mexico," made in Mexico. The peaches, watermelons, cantaloupe, and berries are raised in the Mexican state of Sonora. I have spent large chunks of time in Mexico. I also knew that these fruits, and especially the strawberries, were grown with the aid of chemical fertilizers, chemicals that could and surely would cause great pain to the people working those fields with bare hands. So as I am in my bed popping berries into my dry mouth, I recognize the horrendous fact that people were possibly dying, people I did not personally know, nor ever would; people were dying so that I could eat those terrible berries in a winter city, an unnatural time to be eating strawberries. And they were terrible. Large though they were, at least an inch in circumference, they were tasteless. Below the bright red skin the flesh was colorless, pale white. I did thank my friend profusely, but once she had left, I not only threw the wretched fruit out but vowed I'd never eat Mexican strawberries again unless I personally knew the hands that raised and picked them for the table, and especially those harvested in Sonora.

Directly, I was not the cause of this pain to the workers in Sonora. I'm sufficiently realistic to comprehend this. But my purchasing these fruits decidedly encouraged the use of not only the chemical fertilizers but the deaths of men and women, probably children as well. I was acutely aware that they, the harvesters, could not enjoy the labors as we had when I was a child of those northern meadows, meadows etched by blackeyed susan, purple clover, dandelion; meadows sung to by wrens, larks, bluejays; meadows that in the continuum not only supported our desires for fresh fruit but supported our strengths as a people and as a Nation, for the wild strawberry was given to us by the "little people" who live in a quarry, for the pleasure of eating and to be used in a healing ceremony .

December

Set up the drum.
Winter's on the creek.

Dark men sit in dark kitchens.

139

Words move the air
A neighbor is sick.
Needs prayer.

Women thaw frozen
strawberries.

In the dark...a drum.

Kids hang out
eating burgers
at McDonalds.
The Williams boy
is drunk.

Set up the drum.
Berries thaw,
are crushed,
    fingers stained, and tongues.

Set up the drum.
A neighbor is sick.
Say a prayer.
Dark men sit in dark kitchens.

Wind rattles the moon.

from *The Mama Poems*

While nibbling those horrible cultivated berries I became
enraged with the conglomerate fruit companies, as Pablo Neruda

had years ago, which control the lives of those Mexican farmers who scratch out a meager livelihood from the sands, and I was discouraged with my own self.

Travel has fallen to me easily, I'm sure, as a result of all those early childhood shiftings, and also because at the age of eleven years I was taken by my mother—then legally separated from my father—to live in Bayonne, New Jersey. I stayed in that oil-refining town better than a year. I had many troubles there but the major problem centered at school. I despised every aspect of it. I was, indeed, made to feel I was not only different from the other students but inferior on all accounts. Because of this I refused to attend school/ classes and spent my time either in the local park hiding away or at a candy store that was then called "Jelly Bean," or took flight by bus to Manhattan across the Hudson River with the monies my mother gave me to buy lunch. I can't recall precisely how many days now, but I skipped school a sufficient number, a number dangerously high, enough to bring me before a judge who recommended a reform school for truant boys. My father saved me from that fate and brought me back to northern New York. From high school I returned as often as finances would allow to New York City, much to my father's chagrin. Finally I hitchhiked to North Carolina, at eighteen or nineteen, to pilgrimage to the Thomas Wolfe shrine in Asheville. From there I hitched farther, to New Orleans, with Mexico as my destination. Money prevented this, and I wandered tired and starving along the Mississippi River up to St. Louis where my eldest sister and her husband lived. I stayed there a few months and then came east to Indianapolis, where I entered Butler University.

This was perhaps the wisest move I have ever made. Fortunately, I came under the spell of a Keats scholar, took numerous courses in both literature and creative writing from him, and at last was blessed by his hands and sent adrift to sink or swim as a writer/poet. Werner Beyer has continued to be a very strong influence on my life and writing. I dare not to this moment type a period to the blank page without wondering if Werner would challenge the punctuation. I also worked at Butler with Roy Marz, who was enjoying some national reputation as a poet. He published frequently in *Poetry* magazine, then most prestigious. Roy did not hold as high a degree of respect for my creative efforts as did Werner Beyer, though he did suggest I try my hand at fiction. He felt I struggled under enormous difficulties with poetry, as did John Crowe Ransom, then editor of the famous *Kenyon Review*. Ransom felt I lacked a sense of rhythm. Roy felt my poems lacked not only depth but a classical stance. Little did either poets or teachers ever suspect that European classical poetry might not be my forte.

Under erratic conditions I left Indianapolis, with my father's aid, and returned once more to northern New York, where eventually I enrolled in St. Lawrence University, which had an extension in Watertown. I worked there with Douglas Angus, the novelist, who encouraged me back to poetry and away from fiction. How the young are shifted by whatever prevailing winds! I then made a decision to enter Columbia University in New York City-much to my father's pleasure. I took the entrance exam, which proved extremely difficult, passed and was admitted to the university. However, that was in April of 1957. I never registered. That winter next I enrolled in New York University, deciding it was more important to me to study with Louise Bogan, who taught there then. It proved another wise choice. Louise encouraged my poetry. Her tragic spirit and advice stay with me still. Her suggestions remain constant at my pencil's movement across a blank notebook. At this time my first collection, *Dead Letters Sent* (1958), was published. I remained in New York for approximately six years and then traveled south to Mexico for a brief time. A year later I returned and worked for a great length of time with Willard Motley, the black novelist, author of the very famous best seller *Knock on Any Door*. Willard, a most undisciplined writer, oddly taught me discipline. Rise in the morning, accept the challenge of the blank sheet of paper, and write. Finish the day with a composition: a poem, an essay, a story, or at least a book review or an entry into a journal.

Willard died in 1965, at which time I was living in the U.S. Virgin Islands—St. Thomas, to be exact—not exactly beachcombing but close to it. I drank heavily there, nightly, and wrote practically nothing, though I did complete one poem and proudly saw it appear in the *New York Times*—a major publication for me at that time. Eventually I was rescued from the beach bars of St. Thomas by friends who flew down to the island to boldly retrieve me bodily. I stayed briefly in New York. I appeared on a cold December morning off an airplane in Chicago, where I took a job with the *Chicago Sun* which I held exactly one year. I made my return to New York City in 1967, found an apartment in Brooklyn, and have remained nesting there since. Needing employment, I was fortunate through friends to land a job as a French waiter in a chic discoteque on Park Avenue, where I worked for some six years. I began writing prolifically while in Chicago and continued this, for me, prodigious output. It was not until seventeen years after the publication of *Dead Letters Sent* that my next chapbook was printed: *I Am the Sun*. It originally appeared in *Akwesasne Notes*.

I commenced publishing poems regularly in the *Notes*, which led to my first appearance in an anthology (edited by Walter

Lowenfels), *From the Belly of the Shark*. Since then I have been very active as writer, editor and coordinator, even a college professor. I'm sure Werner Beyer would blanch were he to learn of that fate—my being a teacher. Wemer counseled that I should stay as far away from academia as possible, that it was no place for a writer, that it was suicide. I have concurred with him for thirty years. But so, too, is alcohol suicide for the writer—or for this writer, at least. I gave up booze in 1974 when I suffered a heart attack.

Since then I have continued to travel across "turtle's back," perhaps looking for the cherry blossoms or Alaska, still hunting song and words, right up to this morning where I sit at the window looking out at the birch, the yellowing tamarack, looking toward Mt. Baker rising outside the village of Saranac Lake, a town in which nearly a hundred years ago another poet/ novelist made his home. Robert Louis Stevenson composed his novel *The Master of Ballantrae* and a few short fictions here. Perhaps because his "cottage" is a short walk along the edge of the hill and because I feel his presence, I'm able to sit here at this machine and type out these few facts and figures of my life.

In the north country, either in the mountains or at Akwesasne, it has been diffcult for me to write well. There has been little need. The mountains are here. I live amongst them and with the birch outside my door, the white pine, and my friend Ray Fadden's "bears." I can hear the loons, the Canadian geese flying south to winter; I see mallards and lilies on Turtle Pond; I smell the clarity of air, and await the snow surely to come. All the elements important to my poems, to my life, surround me presently-even the knowledge that wild strawberry vines are deeply embedded in the earth sleeping until spring and June sun. Akwesasne is a mere seventy miles north: Akwesasne where my granddaughter lives with her mother and father/poet Rokwaho, where my ties remain strong, and where my summers are savored.

> is summer this bear
>> home this tamarack
> are these wild berries song
>
> ...
>
> is summer this wolf
>
> ...
>
> is summer this turtle
>
> ...
>
> is summer this tongue
>> home this cedar

from *Is Summer This Bear*
(Chauncey Press, 1985)

A Mohawk Poet on the Road

"This impression was confirmed and deepened
as I traveled along. America is no place for an
artist; to be an artist is to be a moral leper, an
economic misfit, a social liability. A corn-fed
hog enjoys a better life than a creative writer,
painter or musician. To be a rabbit is better
still..."

–Henry Miller
The Air-Conditioned Nightmare

"...No! I'm not a Shaman!"

–M.K.

Without a doubt, reading tours are arranged to sell an author's
book(s). Few poets, indeed, can garner profits at the bookstore,
especially poets published by small or alternative presses. In
recent times, perhaps, only Dylan Thomas and Sylvia Plath have
been near-best sellers. Even Robert Bly, Gary Synder, Denise
Levertov, Allen Ginsberg, and Robert Duncan do not close in on
the charts of the *New York Times* or *Chigago Tribune*. It has been

said that Duncan, a leading poet in this country, sells no more than ten thousand copies of a given title. Other equally impressive names sell far less. Most small press publishers print no more than 1,500 copies in a run, but usually it is a testy 500, or perhaps a small 250 copy run. There are no riches in these numbers. The poet, usually, is utterly sincere in the approach to the platform. The reading itself is rarely suspect, but this ceremony to express and communicate offers the writer an opportunity to "work" the audience with his or her performance and charisma to sell books. Amiri Baraka, for example, is an incredible performer on the platform, and once he has swayed an audience, he could probably sell his socks. Then there are those writers who refuse to read from their publications and instead read from a manuscript. It's unlikely that they sell many, if any, books.

When I travel I carry not only my own books, but also those of the two presses and the magazine with which I'm presently involved. It is necessary to carry cartons of materials and to ship books ahead, as well. I'm usually toting a considerably lighter bundle of luggage when I return home. This commerce does not discredit the poet. In fact, in my opinion, the author rises to another plane. Selling books takes nearly as much energy from the author as it does from the publisher, who more than likely is printing from grant money from the N.E.A., a State Arts Council, or a private foundation. Grants have always been meager, even in the best of economic times. In the production budget of a small/alternative press there is practically no portion allowed for promotion. Monies must go to printing and typesetting. If the publisher is fortunate he can obtain a trade ad with another publisher or possibly an advance review, but both are rare. Occasionally, and particularly, if the press is located in a large metropolitan area, the publisher can promote by having either the poet interviewed or the book blurbed by a radio dj. Adam Miller has been extremely helpful in this method on his program at KPFA in Berkeley, as has Judy Simmons on her WBLS show and various people on WBAI, both of which are located in New York City. They are generous people, but they are writers themselves and understand the seemingly insurmountable problems in promotion and distribution.

All publishers are eager for their poets to go "on the road," though few poets have either the inclination, energy, or, most important, the time for a long series of one-night stands. And that is what it amounts to: one nighters with hurried sleep—often on floors, in train stations, on Greyhound buses— or no sleep at all, thriving on gallons of black coffee and the sturdy arms of friends and coordinators. It's rough. One two-month trip can wheel you into a hospital, be the grounds for divorce, result in the loss of employment, or the loss of an apartment due to an illegal sublease. It might even assure you a cell in debtor's prison. You do not always return home with a bucketful of California gold. You simply do not always make money. Your expenses are not always met or covered.

Yet, on a more positive side, you make numerous new friends, you see the country from Greyhound's green, sometimes finger-smudged window, you are treated to many dinner parties, some a bore, and if you are a gifted reader you may sell books. If you are lucky to sell enough, you shall not only receive the endearment of your publisher but possibly a contract for your new collection as well.

The vicissitudes are multi; the pleasures minimal unless you are a masochist, enjoy hang-ups, are not frustrated easily and can handle various confrontations with ego tucked safely away in the totebag. This is a tremendous problem: safe-keeping the ego, which back home in your own space is nourished daily by fan letters, book reviews, the encouragement of mother, and blurbs written by friends for your books' dust jackets.

The very first insult your ego meets is usually proffered by the English Department. You're feeling glorious. The University of Cat Food is most desirous that you come to the campus. The department has $250.00 for honorarium. An instructor in the department has read your book and consequently would like to have a private evening with you. So a reading is put together. You arrive in Altuna already exhausted from Pittsburgh; you have had no sleep for days, a slice of cold pizza to eat, your feet ache, you've heard your wife is filing for separation, your oldest daughter has run off with a mechanic, your youngest son has dropped out on angel dust, and your home town has been besmirched with PCBs, but the ego is high. The bookstore reading in Pittsburgh was very well attended by thirty aficionados, and you have not only sold three copies of your latest collection but have been promised publication in a new magazine by an editor who has more carnal thoughts than printing your recent verse. It was flattering to be chased around the living-room couch, but, in breathless middle age, you did not give in to those torrid advances. You managed the heaves from the dinner wine, and were spared.

Anyway, Pittsburgh was just sensational. The local newspaper printed one inch on your appearance in town. A radio d.j. blurbed your reading. The bookstore placed a single copy of your new book in the left corner of the side window. Educational TV called just before you boarded the bus to say they'd like to interview you on camera the following week, when you would, of course, be far off in Arizona. OK. You have arrived in Altuna. No one at the depot to meet you. The instructor at the University of

Cat Food has been detained—by papers he has to grade, he says on the phone. You hobble to his house, or to a coffee shop he's directed you to—in a snow storm. It's closed. The bar next door is open. Perhaps it sells coffee...unless you booze.

Your impresario comes to collect you finally two hours later. You still have had no sleep, no food except for either four bottles of beer or four coffees and two bags of very salty pretzels. It is eight o'clock. Your reading is scheduled at eight o'clock. The instructor drives you over sheets of ice in the still raging blizzard. He has lost his glasses but insists you will arrive at the auditorium—or the lounge, if you are considered a very minor poet—on time. Fate again spares you. The Datsun hit only one snow drift and you were hefty enough to dislodge the car while the driver revved up the motor. Though he remembers which building the reading is to be held in, he doesn't know where it's located on campus, and there are no students milling around the streets in the storm to question. Providence hears your curses and responds with a driver of a garbage truck, who sends you off in the correct direction. You arrive at eight-thirty.

Two elderly ladies, obviously neither students nor faculty members, are shivering in a rather drafty lounge best described as "like an ice box". Because there are none in sight, you petition verbally for a podium, a glass of water, and a reading lamp, and...where is the audience? You feel embarrassment spread hotly across your face while spreading out your books for sale, but you've promised your publisher Two students wander in, one holding a copy of Rimbaud, the other a well-worn paperback of Diane DePrima's *Loba*. Your host continues to reassure you that the entire Literature Department, the professors that is, will momentarily arrive. And, of course, the Creative Writing people will appear as well. There are seats for sixty-five people. Thus far four are occupied. The clock hands are pushing eight-forty-five. Five more frozen figures enter the lounge, two with fixed smiles, the other three irritated...remember the storm. Another arrives, then two more. The instructor, your host, beams with an "I told you so" smirk.

To kill time, he introduces you to the matronly ladies. One is his aunt and the other her best friend. They both exclaim their adoration for Robert Frost. A bearded young man enters and approaches you with extended arms to embrace you. You wonder where you have met before. "Mr. Ginsberg," he stammers, "we Creative Writing students are wowed with your appearance at the University of Cat Food." You bungle and flush, want to pull out a knife to stab him through the heart. You are expected to stand up under a deluge of epithets and flattery for at least a half-hour.

There are now twenty-two people in the room, none of whom looks like a potential book buyer. You are introduced. The instructor reads from his review of your latest book, and mistakenly says you live in Berkeley not Brooklyn. Placing sweaty hands on the podium you correct the mistake, attempting a joke which falls flat, and commence the reading of sixteen or seventeen poems from your very best work. You have chosen these poems because they have the tendency to move/ change heads, and they are oral poems. In the business they are called "up poems." Some are strongly political; you must attack the government on campuses as students seem to enjoy getting their elders. You read a poem about your grey-haired mother; you read a haw-haw poem about your dog's parlor trick, you read a poem dealing with the state of Pennsylvania and the crime scene in New York City, and one about travelling cross country, then one on massacres of Indians by the cavalry. Naturally, the dog poem attracts the most attention, even though while you were reading it the janitor entered and clanged his broom on the wastebaskets, suggesting we vacate so he can go home to Archie Bunker. You announce the last poem and a thunderous applause greets your words. You read. A few hands clap. You are then rushed by the audience, though a few, in the words of my good friend, Wendy Rose, elbow you out of the way. One student asks for a copy of your latest book, *Gunslinger*. You perspire while admitting you didn't write that book. In all you sell six books and one copy of the magazine you co-edit. Three of the six books you sold you did not write but *did* publish, one by Amiri Baraka and two by Peter Blue Cloud. They are paid for by a check which will probably bounce. The room clears fast.

The professor is now eagerly concerned about getting rid of you and dumping you off at the bus depot. You inquire about your honorarium which is met with a blank stare. Oh, yes, yes, it's in the mail. You say that it can't be in the mail as you have yet to sign a contract. Well, that's in the mail also. It will be at your home when you return—but he still believes you live in Berkeley. You are accustomed to departmental bureaucratic bungles. It will take a half year for the check to arrive in your mail box.

I have been describing the very worst possible situations—with the exception of arriving and discovering to your heated, chagrined annoyance that you have either been cancelled, for a juggler, without prior warning or you have the wrong date. These things actually do occur, so you have to be prepared for the awful so that you may enjoy the best.

But we're running far ahead of the story by several weeks. The best way, naturally, to schedule a tour is via the most capable hands of booking agents—who are as scarce to poets as ice in the Gobi Desert. An agent acts as buffer when a coordinator does not know your work, name, or performance, and does not consider you worth the fifty bucks for a classroom reading, or holds a personal grudge because once you rejected his poetry for the magazine you edit. We often feel, justifiably, dumped upon when denied a reading—often for weird reasons. Being small press/ alternative press poets without conglomerate monies backing our publications, we can't be known to millions. We are not invited to the Jay Leno Show, the White House, nor are reported on in the *National Inquirer,* though occasionally *The Village Voice* may give your performance a "pick of the week." Few poets are household names. Allen Ginsberg is about the only poet who might qualify for this honor. Few hum your tunes while doing the supper dishes or trill your notes while cutting the backyard grass. There are numerous poets well received/reviewed in the various national periodicals, highly respected by colleagues, and who have created major work but have absolutely no value to the general public. Ntozake Shange is not known for her poetry but for her Broadway hit: *For Colored Girls.* There are poets who, in the literary community, are considered superstars and receive enormous fees for public appearances, especially upon receiving high awards such as the Pulitzer or Nobel prizes, but to Mrs. Jones and Mr. Smith they are lazy bums, better off peddling milk and off the "dole." They aren't Clash or The Rolling Stones. They don't have the clout of G. Gordon Liddy, who I once followed into St. Louis University. He was given a staggering figure as honorarium; I was proffered a pittance that was fought for tooth and nail by the instructor who brought me to the campus. After all, television was not making a film of my life, I hadn't written a best seller, nor was I a criminal convicted in one of the most sensational trials in American history. The workshops have insisted that everyone can write poetry, but everyone can't be involved with Watergate. Is it my suggestion that all touring poets first take up habitation in a federal jail cell? Not exactly. Consider the times: social tastes are decadent, clowns can become senators and B-movie actors can rise to be statesmen and presidents. The fall of the Roman Empire had nothing on us. You have only to read Robert Graves' *I Claudius* to see the parallels. There are poets who could probably be plasticised and promoted by Madison Avenue for public display and consumption. There's a coterie of poets who are as insincere, dishonest and generally corrupt as any other group in the country, interested only in the dollar bill, publication, adoration. But the true poet's chief concern is the construction/creation of the poem, either on the page or the oral platform. Nothing less. Some poets, and I am one, actually enjoy the public performance of their work. Having been in the audience of Joy Harjo, Helen Adam, Jerome Rothenberg, John Weiners, Amiri Baraka, and Judy Grahn, among others, I am aware of the personal rewards, the enjoyment of entertaining an audience. These poets are performers as well as very fine writers. It's the silly young preppies—even though some are old enough to be emeritus—who flounce rear-ends in designer jeans across a platform, dangling a smile worthy of Hollywood before a group of students—that I would tar and feather. These are the "poets" who can never decide which poems to read because, well, they are all just so good, and we'll just love 'em all, including the one written on the spot. They read twaddle which would make the angels turn in their wings and halos. Then there is the drunk poet. Sometimes the beer is lifted in the chill horror of absolute fear/stage fright; others are encouraged by their cult audiences in this disgusting gimmick. Reading one's poems to a live audience is not easy, even when you have the utmost confidence in the poem on the page. Sometimes a beer can help you climb the steps, or black coffee support a shaking voice. But to trip over your own feet climbing those stairs in a totally drunken stupor is not only degrading to the poet's work, but an insult to the audience. At times, self respect would almost appear out of fashion.

Audiences differ greatly. Once in Sacramento I did a gig with Ceasar Chavez for a congress of Catholic Bishops which was televised nationally on all three networks. The auditorium audience of five to six hundred people had not come to hear poetry, and obviously I was out of place. I gave a reading at Turtle, the Native American Center for the Arts in Niagara Falls, N.Y., where I had been led to believe that I was to read for the Indian people of the community. To my confused disbelief, I was booked as a tourist attraction and was an exhibition for the guided tour. Even the reporter/photographer who covered the event for the Buffalo *Evening News* was not only dismayed and perplexed but so embarrassed he did not run the story. In the winter of 1981 I gave a reading for fifteen inmates at the Bellevue Hospital Prison in NYC. It was pure pleasure. The men seemed to accept my reading with enthusiastic delight. One young man wrote me a poem during the performance; others wanted to know where they could buy copies of my work. In that audience there were at least three Spanish speaking men who could not understand a word of English. Yet, they applauded the loudest. They were interested and appreciative.

People attend a poetry reading for various reasons, not all complimentary to the poet. After a reading in Boston, my host received a phone call from a stranger who claimed that it was not possible to attend the night before but had never slept with an "Indian poet" and would like to give it a try even though the caller was sure it would be a lousy lay. My host flushed brilliantly and refused the offer.

The toughest audience to please is one composed of fellow poets whose ears and eyes criticize your every sound, word, movement and can't find paws to show appreciation with slight applause. This audience wouldn't be caught dead purchasing a copy of the reading poet's newest or oldest book. Everyone knows it should be given away free, or at least exchanged for a copy of their book.

Which is the best audience, the most appreciative? Is there such a breed? Does it have to consist of a small crowd composed of your mother, two friends, an old high school sweetheart, a drunk who fell in off the cold street, and obligated neighbors? No. The best audience is composed of ordinary people: the inmate who wrote the poem at Bellevue; the Tuscarora woman at the Black Hills Alliance Benefit in Buffalo who said now she could go home and write some poems; the young student at Sacramento who bought a book though she could ill afford it; the man at Duff's in St. Louis who had nothing to offer but gifted me with a twig of sage in exchange for the oral poems; the shop-keeper in Brooklyn who asked to come to her bake shop to read in order to attract some attention to a failing business; the University of California at San Diego instructor who wrote saying my reading had saved her job because upon the day of my presentation her students were evaluating her performance as a teacher; the basketball student in that same class who hugged me to his jogging suit exclaiming that I was the best damn thing he'd had in his academic career; the young woman at Navajo Community College who presented me with two hawk feathers which had special powers and had belonged to her grandfather; the poet and his beautiful wife who brought a container of corn soup and a packet of Iroquois corn bread to make me feel at home and later became good friends; Harold Iron Shield and his friends who honored my work with a reception and an honor drum in St. Louis; the student who not only bought $25.00 worth of my books but convinced the college bookstore to stock the books; my friends who have given beds, and suppers, and car rides; Arthur Murata, not a poet himself, who over the years has not only carted the body from airport to bus station to auditoriums, but has sat through many and many a boring night hearing the same poems read countless times; my darling friend, Wanda McCaddon, who has hosted me thousands of times in foul weather and fair. People. Yes, it's the common people who make your trip successful. They pay the admittance, buy the book, coerce students to attend the readings, call the doctor when you collapse on their living-room floor, get your shoes repaired, run back for your glasses when you've left them on the kitchen sink, take you to Tijuana for a fling at bargaining for Mexican blankets, take a day off from work to show you around Honeoye Falls, or Seattle, or Vancouver, or Chico, or Canyon DeChelly, or Cahoki Mounds, or even O'Hare airport. They wash your dirty Levi's, know the best rib house in Albuquerque, the best Mexican food in St. Louis, the finest Chinese cuisine in Iowa City, the best gooseberry pie in Butte, stock the best French coffee for you, pick up tabs, and bend—bend to nearly your every wish, comfort, and demand. And a travelling poet can have great demands, sometimes nearly impossible, often selfish and incomprehensible.

In the center of Montana you come to believe you are a travelling medicine show, a phony doctor selling phonier snake oil for castritus with your fixed smile, and your smooth remark to everything everyone says: "Thanks for coming." Usually you are too exhausted to say much more. When you get back home you're forced to write new poems to prove to yourself that you are human, still human, capable of true feeling with some depth, are sensitive to others and their misery or joy.

On October 25th you board Am-Trak for Rochester, the first stop. Next come Buffalo and Olean and Niagara Falls and then the great open spaces to finally arrive in golden California. Between those points you hit St. Louis, Iowa City, Albuquerque, San Diego, Los Angeles, Green Bay, WI, and towns you've forgotten. December 26th, exactly two months later, you arrive home to be greeted by an angry cat, Sula, who refuses to recognize your scent. It takes nearly three days for her to cuddle. She doesn't care that you have visited forty book stores, sold two thousand dollars worth of books, given forty-five readings, rapped with thousands of people, journeyed by Greyhound ten thousand miles, made friends and enemies, left your favorite wine-colored shirt someplace out on the prairie, worn out your tennis shoes, and perhaps worn out your welcome as well. All the cat, Sula, knows is that you've been gone a long time, and it's been lonely. She doesn't realize that you, too, have had lonely nights and days on the road, and now want to roll up into a gunny sack or shape into a couch-potato before the tv and snore across the eastern winter.

It's been good, real good, but taxing—to say the least.

> *"And now," he said, "I am going to tell you the story of Pnin rising to address the Cremona Women's club and discovering he had brought the wrong lecture."*
>
> —Vladimir Nabokov
> *Pnin*

1976

TREMOLO

In the beginning there was only the Spirit World high above dark waters. It was a beautiful and peaceful world, a world without sorrow, pain or death. People were content until a virgin woman became pregnant. Nearing her term and while walking across the Spirit World, anxious and pleased, she happened upon a small hole in the floor of the Spirit World where none had been before. She stopped and looked into the hole, which grew wider and rounder as she peered into the emptiness of the abyss. She bent and looked deeper and as she did she fell, though there are those who say her impatient brother/husband, the Creator, pushed her and covered the hole with a great elm tree. She fell toward the dark waters. Suddenly water birds came to her rescue: mallard, crane, grebe, heron and loon. These beautiful and considerate birds banded together and formed a blanket of wings to catch her fall. Slowly the birds brought her down to the dark waters and they called Turtle, listlessly waiting in the mud on the bottom of the dark sea. Turtle rose from the mud and surfaced to accept Sky Woman on his shell. Soon she gave birth to a girl child who in years to come gave birth to twin boys who together created all the beauty of this world on Turtle's shell. The water birds have always been respected by the Turtle-people since then: heron, grebe, and particularly loon, whose tremolo is heard to this moment coming from across a wide lake, dark and smooth.

(from the Mohawk Creation Story)

Listen! Hear the old coyote howl on the mountain; listen to the singing of the wood thrush; shiver to the hoot of owls; duck from swooping bats chasing black flies. We in this northern clime are fortunate to live among the indigenous animals and birds who walk the dark of night and light of day, to have the shine of fish in near-clean waters—salmon, pike, rainbow trout—and the beauty of water and air fowl—mallards, red-tail hawk, eagle, kingfisher—and listen to the cry of the loon.

I am Mohawk. I was born not far from the Adirondack Mountains, in the foothills in Northern New York State, and came to know the privilege of this "forever wild," this paradise of ancient mountains, lakes, forests and winters of brutal cold. My father had been a hunter and a fisherman and my sights were early placed to the creatures of the woods and streams through the stories he told of the four-leggeds, the wingeds and those of the waters and how they all came to be. As a boy I canoed the rivers and lakes, trekked pine and spruce woods sighting red fox or raccoon. I was overjoyed spotting a rainbow trout circling a shallow pool. I learned the verdure as well: wild iris, witchhopple, chokecherry, hemlock, hickory, blackberry and wild strawberry.

Camping, canoeing, swimming were the highlights of summer; sledding, skiing and skating were the joys of winter. Traipsing through woods or trekking rivers, I taught myself that killing the various creatures was not necessary. I hunted without a gun, fished without a hook and pole. My trophies came home in the memory or on a piece of paper, as a poem or outline of a story.

And then, after high school, I left. My father repeatedly told me that there was no place in the world as beautiful as our north and our mountains. As a young man, of course, I didn't believe him. I traveled and lived in foreign lands and distant states, worked in large cities, went to college in the Midwest and seemed to forget or ignore the North Country, and in the exodus took for granted that life in that area would continue and be the same should I ever decide to return. The wing of the cardinal, bellow of a moose, howl of the wolf and flight of the pheasant would always be there.

I fear I was not the only one to take the north and the many creatures for granted. People who lived there paid little attention to the birds, the fish, the animals, the greens, the cry of the loon—a sign that the bird was there breeding and hatching, vibrant and resilient in the waters of Adirondack lakes—until acid rain took its tragic toll of water and plant life. It was thought the loon as well as the red fox or beaver was as common as wood anemone or red trillium.

I left the north for college and then work. My sojourn was long. I returned to my natal waters only for weddings and funerals, beginnings and endings, where conversations never rose above the din of laughter, the tears, or the bitterness, and I never lingered long. I wasn't there long enough to observe changes in the flora and fauna: death of the Dutch elm, demise of the magnificent salmon on which I supped many a night as a small child; the slow disappearance of that gorgeous wild flower that some came to think of as the stink flower, the blood trillium. Living in Chicago or San Francisco or New York City, I had little thought of home with the exception that cousin George was recently married for the third time and Aunt Millie had passed the January before last. I did not come back north for high school reunions, though I doubt anyone knew my address to post an invitation.

And then retirement began to loom in my fears, and I began to wonder if the city was where I wished to stay. I began to hear the hoot of the owl and the caw of the crow in my sleep; the scent of milkweed and honeysuckle resurfaced from my memory. I pondered going home, home to the north, but could I give up Broadway shows, the Metropolitan Museum, lunch at good bistros, walks on the Brooklyn Heights Promenade, Friday night jazz concerts at South Street Seaport Museum. Was I ready to forfeit these humanities for country picnics, church bazaars, long and icy winter nights when it would be impossible to drive into town for a movie? Was I ready for shoveling snow and mowing lawns?

Despite these misgivings, there came a time when it was common to conjure dreams of home in the north and remember the potluck suppers, cross-country skiing, Winter Carnival in Saranac Lake, summer concerts in Lake Placid's band shell, the hike up Mt. Jo or Scarface, or that two-day trek up the beauties of Mt. MacKenzie. I had forgotten black flies, for sense has told them for centuries to stay out of big cities, something which they never told their cousin, the mosquito. I'd forgotten when to water the tomatoes, let alone which kind of soil they grow in, or whether they need morning or late-day sun. I had forgotten that the fisher had returned to its natural habitat: meadows and conifer woods. I didn't know the black bear could now be hunted, that deer carry Lyme disease, that the loon cries like a child, that eagles have been spotted on a high spire of a white pine shored on Lake Flower, that moose have come home to the Adirondacks.

It would take time to get back into the proverbial saddle, I thought. But the bags were packed, the house sold, the cat in her carrier. Friends had been warned to make sure the apple pie is in the oven, the chicken and biscuits ready for the famished traveler, a traveler who decided that Broadway shows and bistros were not important to the good life. I had a last Guiness Stout with the boys from the department. The university would run quite well without me. In fact, I could recommend a successor, an expert in Egyptology, or economics, or teacher arts. I'm gone. Gone. Kissed old Central Park goodbye; leaned a tear against the old Heights brownstone, wondering if anyone will ever care to screw in a plaque saying I lived there for twenty years.

And the next thing I know, I'm on the peak of Mt. Jo, Heart Lake below, a jug of black coffee in my tote, field glasses hanging down my chest, resting on my middle-aged paunch, my heavy breathing from the climb slowly changing into a deep prolonged sigh at the sight of the sublime: off, in the far distance, my gaze embraces Indian Pass, Mt. Marcy, tall Algonquin, the other high peaks bathed in a glow of falling sunlight and a pure haze that I had forgotten ever existed.

Suddenly the twilight is shattered by a weird, uncanny noise: a child lost in the woods or in danger on a mountain ledge. The cry tears the silence, the ambiance. What will I do? Don't panic. How can I help that child in such danger?

I chuckle at my own miserable memory. It isn't a child lost in the brush, caught on a ledge, thirsty. It is the wail of a water bird. Spring light is falling upon Heart Lake and a final ray of sun clutches the head of a loon. It cries, calls out to a fledgling swimming a quarter of a mile off. It is time for night. I gaze down at the black dot on the lake, and then, knowing it is time for me, too, to enter the tribal cave, I lope down Mt. Jo's rugged slope and go home to flames in the fireplace and a huge pot of stew.

Rediscovering the natal waters, reacquainting the memory, is a delightful, exciting education. I am getting to know the blue flag, rainbow trout, and habits of grey fox, raccoon, and woodpecker again. I am discovering where the raspberries ripen on the bush, the place where bear has not eaten all the blueberries, where the lakes are, which mountain can be climbed in an afternoon, the best hiking trails. Watching for cardinals or simply listening for crows, trying to outsmart black flies and mosquitoes, I am making friends of old acquaintances.

I'm home at last in the north. From my sun porch window I view Scarface, Haystack, MacKenzie, with Whiteface towering beyond. Cousins have come with hands extended for shaking. Friends stop off with a rhubarb pie, applesauce, homemade bread, or a casserole of scalloped potatoes. My nature books are separated out from cookbooks, poetry and fiction. I have a new cat and long for a black labrador. I settle in to listen for the old coyote singing on the hill and watch for a wolf or bobcat scratching a beech tree, or perhaps a fisher hiding in the thick branches of a hemlock. I'm ready for a canoe paddle.

August, Sunday morning. Bob lifts his canoe on top of his Isuzu. I pack a thermos of coffee. The scent of blackberries is in the air. Black flies have had sufficient human blood to disappear. Woods are noisy with kit raccoons trampling the underbrush. The sun stands momentarily behind Little Burn Mountain. The lake below is dotted with canoes and motor boats. Three young boys fish at the dam on Lake Flower where beyond it becomes once again the River Saranac, Algonquian for "place of red sumac." The town is fairly still; few cars careen up and down Lake Flower Drive or Main Street; few senior citizens wend their way down the street to church. No sirens blast the air.

Packed and heading down the road, we are as excited as two kids going off to their first circus. The canoe travels well on the van's top. In glee we spot waves of black-eyed Susans just off the road and yarrow just beyond. Other vehicles pass us with canoes or kayaks tied to the roof. They are in a hurry to get to their lake of choice: St. Regis, Tupper or Blue Mountain.

We head for Polliwog Pond, where Bob knows of a cranberry bog he needs to investigate. It's part of a chain, and we'll have to carry the canoe from one pond to another to reach it.

Our first paddle is calm water, smooth as a field of new snow. We are alone. Bob calls out to keep an eye for water birds, especially loon. There isn't a bird in view, only a fallen log or two floating on the water. We do hear the caw of a crow on shore in the deep woods. We see nothing on our several carries from one to another in our chain of ponds—not a fox, or skunk, or squirrel. We see few flowers blooming in this gorgeous August sunlight, only a few trillium plants that hold no blossoms.

We pause occasionally to glance down at mushrooms. We feign picking. We can only guess at the names of the mushrooms, the moss, and the growth on the various felled logs rotting into the earth of the forest floor. This would be a good winter study, we conclude.

On our third carry, to Little Polliwog, we meet three women and a boy just touching shore. We greet them, and the women claim they spotted several loons. Bob and I grow excited. We ask if they have canoed through the cranberry bog. They shake their heads 'no' in bewilderment, apparently not knowing it exists.

We lower the canoe into the warm water and push off. Off to the left, only a short paddle, is Bob's bog. We spend an hour paddling through, looking for signs of cranberries. We spot nothing, not a single berry ripening under what is by now a very warm sun. Nor do we spot any of the loons the women spoke of in such pleasure.

Our last carry is to Polliwog. Atop the esker that separates it from Little Polliwog, we discover a mountain bike trail. We pause to smell the marvelous scents of pine and spruce and detect the smell of burning wood from a camp we cannot see.

A young man rolls out of the woods on a bike. He barely waves. Our comments are strong, bitter, political. We don't want wheels rutting these eskers.

"Well, if he can ride a bike across the rim of this esker, I can eat my Oh Henry candy bar. He'll leave tracks, but I'll take my wrapper out," I say.

Bob nods in agreement, and we steal down the steep incline to the pond. Bob stops and lowers the canoe down gently to the shallow waters. As if to say "be still," he puts a finger to his lips. He hears something that I do not.

"Hear it?" he whispers, barely audible.

Yes, I do—a wail, the sound scientists say loons use to announce their location. It penetrates to the soul, the very essence of being. We could have heard the wail from a mile distant had we been tuned. It is intense.

We stiffen, anticipating revelation. Apprehensive but calm with silent determination, I step down the bank. Fortunately I do not trip on a root or over a rock, but position myself next to Bob, who has sprouted a hundred ears. I am breathless. Our hearts have ceased to beat, though the sugar from the candy bar rumbles in my belly.

"There it is," Bob undertones so quietly I can hardly distinguish his words.

"Where?" I ask.

He points an index finger out to the center of the lake to our left. "There."

A large black dot bobs on the water. Perhaps it has caught our scent on the winds. It lifts and with wings hardly flapping, skims the water for several yards. Then its wings fall to its sides, it emits another wail, and glides away, becoming smaller by the second.

"Quiet," Bob cautions. "Listen. There's another one."

We hear the wail—not quite a tremolo—of a second loon. We can't spot it but its cry comes from our right. Very slowly we slip the canoe into the water, climb aboard, and push off with the help of a paddle. Directly to our right, not fifty yards away, is another loon, not a black dot this time.

The first loon we spotted, perhaps a female, is moving away. But the second—we believe it to be a male—is paddling closer to the canoe. We move quickly out into the lake. The male paddles faster, directly toward our canoe. We float, our paddles raised and dripping teardrops.

The gentle current seems to push the canoe toward the loon. Forces bring us together. He is now a mere twenty feet off, now fifteen, as together we ride farther out onto the pond. The female is moving toward us. She wails, attracts our attention, flies off the surface, scans the lapping waters, alights again and waits our cue. She wails once more and beats her wings to catch our focus. The male is closer to us still. Bob paddles sluggishly, steering off the natural course of the ripples caused by the slight breeze upon the water.

The ripples—something is causing the lake to buckle. It is a fledgling, a young loon from this year's hatch. It dives playfully, abandons care, fearless. Quickly it surfaces, dives once more for a moment and then reappears, bobbing on the surface.

The male floats closer to the active young bird. It does not wail. There is no tremolo, no yodel, no hoot, no sound of throttled fear, danger, or distress. Its red eye, its severe gaze, is focused on the canoe, all its senses intent on our movements, our breathing. We are now eight feet from it.

Farther out, the other loon is flapping wings against the water, splashing hard, making great disturbances and calling out loud wails in her attempt to draw our sight away from the male and the chick. She rises up, flapping the water. The fledgling must be in trouble, great trouble. Yet it bobs on the surface, diving, surfacing, seeming to enjoy its outing on the lake.

We and the male are now maybe six feet apart. We have a profile view. Its eye's curt glance cuts us to the quick. "Know thy friends," it seems to say. And we are probably not its friends. If we were, we would paddle off and leave this bird family in peace to deal with the fledgling's problem in its own manner, its own natural way. We have created an extra strain upon the parents, caused more stress than what this family should bear. It has been said that if a loon is in extreme danger from a predator—and we humans are predators—the powerful stress can cause a massive fatal heart attack.

We humans are the cause of the anxiety. Though the adult male appears calm, in charge of the situation, relaxed and fearless, we know it suffers an agony only the terrified can know.

"Bob, let's shove off. We'd better paddle away from here."

He agrees, and reluctantly, in the very heat of a first and probably last experience such as this, we lower the paddles into the water and move swiftly away from the loon.

We did not have a camera. That day we would have given our right arms, our bank accounts, to have had a camera with us. Yet nothing could capture that moment: the black of the wing, the white of the collar, the tilt of the head, or the rise to the light.

We were alone on that pond with one male adult loon, one female adult and a chick. The male we could have touched with our paddles or possibly our hands as its life and the life of its offspring rested in our minds, our decision, in that fleeting experience. I am thankful that Bob is a gentle and caring human being, that he made the huge decision to paddle away from the loon and the chick, knowing the frightful danger we had placed the birds in.

Why didn't it fly off when we came so close? Why didn't it encourage the chick to fly? We continued asking these questions over and over on our way home. Was it the adult who was sick? It didn't appear to have a broken wing. We couldn't see signs of a bullet or fish hook wound. It appeared healthy. We were sure it was the chick who was in trouble. And yet it, too, appeared healthy, bobbing up and down.

What was wrong? Why didn't it wail or give a tremolo? We have no idea. Some questions invite no answers. Why is the loon sixty million years on this earth on Turtle's back? Why did it aid Sky Woman in her fall from the Iroquois Spirit World? Why does it nest each year in the same spot on its return from the southern seas? Why does it call its mate each year after separation? How has it survived so many millions of years?

That is the mystery and the magic of nature, the gift of the Creator, the Great Spirit.

Monday, town. Down-town: gift shops, windows in the hotel, posters in the frame store, reprint photos in the bank. Loons.

Loons all over town: postcards, posters, t-shirts, sweatshirts, wooden pins, plaster replicas, ties, bolas, hand-painted coffee mugs, plastic plates, china plates, paintings, tote bags, books and books and books, poems, essays—all about the mysterious, private loon.

There is indeed something very special about being born and raised in northern New York, especially in the foothills of the Adirondack Mountains. On a good night you can hear the song of the old coyote on the mountain or the tremolo of the loon passing overhead at twilight.

I, too, am considered a tourist, someone passing through. I wasn't born inside the "blue line." Northwest of the mountains were my natural waters/earth, although I felt attachment to the hills and woods, lands I lived away from for many years. I've come home before it is too late to see the herons, cranes, mallards and kingfisher, hear the cry or song of the loon not as a visitor but as someone who has a natural identity, a natural need to be a part of the north. It was my people, my Sky Woman, whom loon helped to descend safely onto Turtle's back. I have a right to the north, I have a right to the north, home; to hear the song of the crow, growl of the bear, wind in the white pine, the loon.

American Poetry from White Pine Press

BODILY COURSE
Deborah Gorlin
90 pages $12.00 paper
Winner 1996 White Pine Press Poetry Prize

TREEHOUSE: NEW & SELECTED POEMS
William Kloefkorn
224 pages $15.00 paper

CERTAINTY
David Romtvedt
96 pages $12.00 paper

ZOO & CATHEDRAL
Nancy Johnson
80 pages $12.00 paper
Winner 1995 White Pine Press Poetry Prize

DESTINATION ZERO
Sam Hamill
184 pages $15.00 paper
184 pages $25.00 cloth

CLANS OF MANY NATIONS
Peter Blue Cloud
128 pages $14.00 paper

HEARTBEAT GEOGRAPHY
John Brandi
256 pages $15.00 paper

LEAVING EGYPT
Gene Zeiger
80 pages $12.00 paper

WATCH FIRE
Christopher Merrill
192 pages $14.00 paper

BETWEEN TWO RIVERS
Maurice Kenny
168 pages $12.00 paper

TEKONWATONTI: MOLLY BRANT
Maurice Kenny
209 pages $12.00 paper

DRINKING THE TIN CUP DRY
William Kloefkorn
87 pages $8.00 paper

GOING OUT, COMING BACK
William Kloefkorn
96 pages $11.00 paper

JUMPING OUT OF BED
Robert Bly
48 pages $7.00 paper

POETRY: ECOLOGY OF THE SOUL
Joel Oppenheimer
114 pages $7.50 paper

WHY NOT
Joel Oppenheimer
46 pages $7.00 paper

TWO CITIZENS
James Wright
48 pages $8.00 paper

SLEEK FOR THE LONG FLIGHT
William Matthews
80 pages $8.00 paper

WHY I CAME TO JUDEVINE
David Budbill
72 pages $7.00 paper

AZUBAH NYE
Lyle Glazier
56 pages $7.00 paper

SMELL OF EARTH AND CLAY
East Greenland Eskimo Songs
38 pages $5.00 paper

FINE CHINA: TWENTY YEARS OF EARTH'S DAUGHTERS
230 pages $14.00 paper

Poetry in Translation from White Pine Press

THE FOUR QUESTIONS OF MELANCHOLY
Tomaz Salamun
224 pages $15.00 paper

THESE ARE NOT SWEET GIRLS
An Anthology of Poetry by Latin American Women
320 pages $17.00 paper

A GABRIELA MISTRAL READER
277 pages $13.00 paper

ALFONSINA STORNI: SELECTED POEMS
72 pages $8.00 paper

CIRCLES OF MADNESS: MOTHERS OF THE PLAZA DE MAYO
Marjorie Agosín
128 pages $13.00 paper   Bilingual

SARGASSO
Marjorie Agosín
92 pages $12.00 paper   Bilingual

MAREMOTO/SEAQUAKE
Pablo Neruda
64 pages $9.00 paper   Bilingual

THE STONES OF CHILE
Pablo Neruda
98 pages $10.00 paper   Bilingual

VERTICAL POETRY: RECENT POEMS BY ROBERTO JUARROZ
118 pages $11.00 paper   Bilingual

LIGHT AND SHADOWS
Juan Ramon Jimenez
70 pages $9.00 paper

ELEMENTAL POEMS
Tommy Olofsson
70 pages $9.00 paper

FOUR SWEDISH POETS:
STROM, ESPMARK, TRANSTROMER, SJOGREN
131 pages $9.00 paper

NIGHT OPEN
Rolf Jacobsen
221 pages $15.00 paper

SELECTED POEMS OF OLAV HAUGE
92 pages $9.00 paper

TANGLED HAIR
Love Poems of Yosano Akiko
48 pages $7.50 paper   Illustrated

A DRIFTING BOAT
An Anthology of Chinese Zen Poetry
200 pages $15.00 paper

BETWEEN THE FLOATING MIST
Poems of Ryokan
88 pages $12.00 paper

WINE OF ENDLESS LIFE
Taoist Drinking Songs
60 pages $9.00 paper

TANTRIC POETRY OF KUKAI
80 pages $7.00 paper

About White Pine Press

White Pine Press is a non-profit publishing house dedicated to enriching our literary heritage; promoting cultural awareness, understanding, and respect; and, through literature, addressing social and human rights issues. This mission is accomplished by discovering, producing, and marketing to a diverse circle of readers exceptional works of poetry, fiction, non-fiction, and literature in translation from around the world. Through White Pine Press, authors' voices reach out across cultural, ethnic, and gender boundaries to educate and to entertain.

To insure that these voices are heard as widely as possible, White Pine Press arranges author reading tours and speaking engagements at various colleges, universities, organizations, and bookstores throughout the country. White Pine Press works with colleges and public schools to enrich curricula and promotes discussion in the media. Through these efforts, literature extends beyond the books to make a difference in a rapidly changing world.

As a non-profit organization, White Pine Press depends on support from individuals, foundations, and government agencies to bring you this literature that matters—work that might not be published by profit-driven publishing houses. Our grateful thanks to the many individuals who support this effort as Friends of White Pine Press and to the following organizations: Amter Foundation, Ford Foundation, Korean Culture and Arts Foundation, Lannan Foundation, Lila Wallace-Reader's Digest Fund, Margaret L. Wendt Foundation, Mellon Foundation, National Endowment for the Arts, New York State Council on the Arts, Trubar Foundation, Witter Bynner Foundation, the Slovenian Ministry of Culture, The U.S.-Mexico Fund for Culture, and Wellesley College.

Please support White Pine Press' efforts to present voices that promote cultural awareness and increase understanding and respect among diverse populations of the world. Tax-deductible donations can be made to:

White Pine Press
10 Village Square • Fredonia, NY 14063